CRITICAL SPIRITUAL ISSUES

Bridging The Spiritual With
The Psychological

By

David E. Miller, Ph.D., FICPP
Psychologist

Unless otherwise indicated Bible quotations are taken from The NIV Study Bible. Copyright © 1995 by The Zondervan Corporation.

Drury, Keith. "The Anatomy of Adultery," Money, Sex, & Spiritual Power, Indianapolis: Wesley Press, 1992, 45. Used by permission.

Hermiz, Thomas. "Get Rid of All Bitterness," Circleville: Mount of Praise Camp Meeting Sermon, August 1997. Used by permission.

Hermiz, Thomas. "Self Love," Circleville: Mount of Praise Camp Meeting Sermon, August 1997. Used by permission.

Hotle, Marlin, "Forgiveness," Circleville: Mount of Praise Camp Meeting Sermon, August 1998. Used by permission.

Potts, Lonnie. "What Does God's Word Say About Divorce?" Circleville: Crossroads Church Sermon Series, June, 2003. Used by permission.

Xulon Press
www.XulonPress.com

Xulon Press books are available in bookstores everywhere, and on the Web at www.XulonPress.com.

Disclaimer

The names of patients and some descriptions of their characteristics and symptoms have been slightly altered to protect their confidentiality and privacy.

Dedication

This book is dedicated to several people who have played significant roles in motivating and encouraging me to write it. Among them are the many patients who I have treated in my practice over the past several years, sincerely searching for answers to their problems. Their confusion over spiritual issues and the emotions they experienced has demonstrated the need for such a project. My wife, Joy, who consistently upholds me and my patients in prayer; her constant encouragement and support of my ministry to hurting people, provides energy to persevere on those discouraging days that every psychologist in private practice faces from time to time. My children, Scott and his wife, Cara, & Lori and her husband, Adam, who frequently express their encouragement and admiration for their dad's work. Many thanks are due my godly parents, Rev. L.B. and Ruth Miller, who have encouraged me in my practice and supported it as a ministry to God's people. Finally, this book is dedicated to future generations of persons who will search for answers to the problems addressed in this book.

Table of Contents

Chapter 1

What Are The Critical Spiritual Issues Of Today?

As a clinical psychologist, I have had the privilege of treating hundreds of adults, teenagers, children, married couples, and families experiencing emotional problems over the past several years. The range of problems seen within a family practice covers the whole gamut of psychological and emotional difficulties. On any given day, I could begin seeing a couple in marital therapy struggling to correct problems in their marriage and re-ignite the romance that has seemed to disappear. Following that session, I might transition to a family session in an effort to help parents deal with children experiencing hyperactivity, attention deficit disorder, or perhaps acting out teenagers who challenge their parents' love by absolutely rejecting every spiritual value taught and modeled in their home.

Then, there are the normal emotional reactions to stress, loss, disappointment and trauma ranging from major depression to generalized anxiety and panic attacks. The more severe disorders such as schizophrenia, suicidal thoughts, psychotic or delusional thought processes, obsessive-compulsive disorder, eating disorders, victimization from abuse, and a rather extensive continuum of addictive behaviors from substance abuse to pornography and use of internet chat rooms all find their place on the schedule for appointments. These more difficult matters are best handled if they can be tucked in between the less challenging situations involving strong-willed children or irrational fears that can actually be more rewarding in assisting the individual or family reach resolution of the presenting problems.

Throughout the 20 years of practicing as a psychologist, in a range of settings including private practice as well as public mental health facilities and inpatient hospitals, I have seen what appears to be a repetitive pattern of several issues. Although such issues are presented in a variety of ways, the underlying issue can be the same and serves to disrupt or interfere with the patient's desire to achieve that deep settled peace described in scripture and expressed by the lyrics in many of the songs used in worship.

While this list is not exhaustive or even comprehensive in nature, it perhaps addresses twelve (12) primary issues that I would like to term "critical spiritual issues." The reason for this level of significance is quite simple; some important concepts have been misunderstood and at times misrepresented or explained by well meaning people in a manner that has caused confusion for many. As they attempt to apply such concepts in their daily walk, they are left with further confusion and disharmony. Instead of bringing a peace, many have been left with further confusion and stress as they try to make sense and find the relevancy such issues have for their life. Clarification of these very commonly found issues and giving consideration to their application for living a life of holiness can help us reach a deeper level of understanding and thus come closer to an inner contentment that should characterize our walk with God. Still other issues, likely caused by loss, deep hurt, or some other trauma absolutely need resolution of the conflict to reach the peace that God desires for all His children. It is for these reasons that this work is seen as relevant. Through the application of newly learned or clarified principles in one's life, it is our hope that such will help prevent vulnerability to problems that can bring disharmony and ultimately cause symptoms that could require therapeutic intervention.

The critical issues to be addressed in the chapters that follow—all of which have significance to the Christian life are:

Important Boundaries For A Life of Holiness

In a day that the culture promotes having no boundaries since limits might prevent one from finding ultimate fulfillment in life, the Christian finds this popular notion to be extremely dangerous. It is the failure to maintain boundaries that significantly increases one's susceptibility to poor decisions and quite often participation in sin that maintaining basic boundaries would help to prevent. While not becoming obsessed with rigidity and appearing like Pharisees whose public lives did not convey living within the joy of the Lord, Christians need to return to considering the importance of "protective" boundaries. We need protective boundaries in many areas of our personal lives: professional, familial, technological, personal-marital, and even in some of the spiritual aspects.

Anger—Is It Wrong?

Anger has for decades been confusing to people who wish to have a life that reflects Christ. Some would see any expression of anger as sinful, or carnal in nature; these people feel that the expression of any form of anger is displeasing to God and a hindrance to their witness. Anger is an emotion; emotions are God-given attributes, emotions are not sinful. Can anger ever progress to sin? How does one learn to express legitimate anger with a pure heart? What is the difference between anger and what scripture describes as bitterness? These are examples of the multitude of questions that have contributed to the confusion surrounding this normal human attribute. We must gain insight into the emotion of anger; wisdom to help us understand the causal factors of our anger, and ultimately how to resolve issues in a healthy manner—thus achieving victory over it. Resolution of anger can help us find the peace and tranquility that only such inner healing can provide. Failure to resolve it can lead to the devastating effects of bitterness, which without question is sin.

Anxiety—Is It Sin?

Like other emotions, anxiety is an emotional response; it too is a God given attribute that has benefits to our overall emotional well-being. Yet many seem to be overwhelmed with anxiety or even extreme levels of anxiety known as panic attacks. Many people feel that if they become anxious about anything, they are not trusting in God or their faith is weak. How does one interpret the scripture that advocates in Philippians 4:6 "do not be anxious about anything?" If I become anxious, does that mean there is sin in my life? Is anxiety a sign of a weakened faith? Is God trying to get my attention through my fear and discomfort that overwhelms me through anxiety?

Such are the many questions that have characterized the Christian experiencing this problem. Answers, insights, and wisdom for managing this normal emotional response that affects multitudes of Christians can help to reduce the devastation it can produce for those experiencing it.

Proper Self-Esteem vs. Selfish Pride

Perhaps the church in general, in addition to well meaning pastors and laypersons, have not sufficiently addressed the importance of good self-esteem for one's overall healthy emotional adjustment. Too often, self-esteem is equated with selfish pride, thereby thoroughly confusing the God fearing Christian who is seeking God's perfect will for his or her life. James Dobson has often referred to what he terms "an epidemic" of low self esteem within the Church. While we often see this among women, it is probably equally a problem for men; men are just less willing to share their inner most feelings with others. God wants His children to feel positive about themselves for we are created in His image. He has endowed us with significant attributes far above any other part of creation. Accepting one's own attributes and utilizing them for advancing the Kingdom is very different than selfish pride which is carnal in nature. The person with selfish pride has an attitude of getting ahead no matter who they have to step on to reach their goal; this type of pride is sin. Achieving and maintaining good self-esteem is accepting God's blessing to us and enables us to be more fit for accomplishing His call upon our life. Selfish pride is radically different from good self-esteem; and, the confusion that has historically existed among Christian circles concerning these two concepts needs clarification.

Solutions For Dealing With Guilt

Multitudes of people struggle with underlying guilt over either trauma or sin in their lives. While manifesting in a variety of symptoms ranging from major depression and repressed anger or bitterness to excessive anxiety or panic attacks, the source of such pain can be traced to a lack of forgiveness either by God, others, or themselves. Guilt is an overwhelming sense of power-lessness that Satan continues to use as one of his greatest weapons against people who truly are seeking to live victorious lives. Most Christians can intellectually understand that God's shed blood forgives their past sins and that the shed blood of Christ fully covers their past deeds; however, they can still struggle emotionally with a sense of defeat which inhibits their self confidence and joy.

The Importance of Balance and Proper Priorities

Balance in our lives and maintaining proper priorities can prevent many problems resulting when such a balance is not kept. Over-involvement even within church or religious activities, referred by some as "toxic faith," can be as wrong as devotion to secular activities at the exclusion of time set aside for spiritual matters. Over-involvement in any area of our life can become the rationale and serve as an escape from obligations in important areas such as marriage, family, employment, and work within our church. Despite the desire to follow proper priorities, the fast pace we maintain and the demanding society in which we live do not allow sufficient time for everything. Becoming obsessed with any particular area will prevent the balance that God has designed as proper.

We need to learn the essence of Ecclesiastes 3:1, "There is a time for everything, and a season for every activity under heaven."

Good Decision Making

Absolutely no one is invulnerable to poor decision-making; I have and continue to deal with all levels of people including people who are a part of holiness denominations, college graduates of holiness colleges or Bible colleges, people who fulfill leadership roles in the church, and even ordained ministers from time to time. Good decision-making—perhaps better termed as "Godly" decision-making— is not endowed on us when we become Christians. Patients seem to want a formula or technique that will increase their ability to make better decisions and therefore avoid repeating a pattern that has produced stress in their lives. While there are multitudes of theories in the field and literally thousands of self-help books available on this subject, only by learning how to "test the spirits" will we lower our human vulnerability in this essential area of our life.

The Importance Of Learning How To Forgive

Perhaps one of the greatest misunderstood concepts within the church and the care-giving fields ministering to the emotional healing of people is the process of forgiveness. Although not intentionally, the church has sometimes caused more confusion for those struggling with forgiveness than it has helped; unfortunately, at times well meaning churches or church leaders have severely damaged people seriously seeking counsel in this area. The lack of forgiveness of others or oneself often leads to bitterness which scripture warns against in Ephesians 4:31 "Get rid of all bitterness ... ." While looking at forgiveness from a spiritual perspective can be somewhat different than from a clinical one, the two approaches are not incompatible. Forgiveness is a two step-process, much like the second work of grace we know as "holiness". There is the decision to forgive just as in sanctification we have a "crisis experience" when we decide to surrender our all to God. After this crisis experience, which is our decision for sanctification, the surrendered Christian begins a process of becoming holy through what we refer to as "progressive sanctification." In forgiveness, there is the decision to forgive, and then there is a process of resolving this past hurt or pain that takes place over time. Unlike Godly forgiveness of our sins, as human beings, we do not have the capacity to forget things we have forgiven. While failing to put these things out of our memory entirely, we can reach a resolution that prevents further damage that inhibits the peace that God can provide through His grace.

Perfectionism—Is It An Emotional Problem Or A Sign Of Holiness?

For a number of years there has existed confusion within the holiness denominations about what is popularly referred to as "Christian Perfection". While we are called to be holy and scripture warns that "without holiness no one will see the Lord" (Hebrews 12:14), does this mean we must be perfect? Matthew 5:48 exhorts "be perfect ... as your heavenly Father is perfect." How can one be perfect in this earthen vessel? Can we be prone to human error or mistakes and still be perfect in heart? Do some use this "earthen vessel" concept to justify or excuse their sin? Perhaps further elaboration on what holiness is and what it is not, and what it will do and what it will not do in one's life might add clarification, thus helping one make application within their life. When does our pursuit of becoming more perfect or growing into the "perfection" promoted as holiness become an emotional problem known as obsessive-compulsive disorder? Does God expect or is He pleased with such an exaggeration of our pursuit of perfection? Can this issue be used by Satan to dishearten the sincere child of God who is seeking to grow in what holiness denominations refer to as "progressive" sanctification?

Sexual Identity Problems—Is There A Cause? What's The Cure?

Sexual identity problems, once viewed even by public institutions such as American Psychological Association (APA) and

American Medical Association (AMA) as disorders, are now seen as "sexual preference" and one's individual right to practice his or her sexual desires in any manner they like. While scripture has always viewed homosexuality as sin, has the church begun to compromise its interpretation of this carnal and perverted lifestyle? Why are churches now seeing an increase of people who advocate this behavior and maintain they are Christians? Is homosexuality caused genetically or is it like other sins, a choice made by the individual? What are the causes from a spiritual perspective? And even more important, what are the solutions for those who seem confused by this issue in their life? What should be our view as Christians in ministering to such individuals? Sexual identity issues can be a very serious problem with many complexities and without simple or easy answers; however, insights of the causal factors can help one reach resolution and obtain the God ordained sexuality that He designed in His creation for mankind.

Internet Pornography—Newest Threat To The Church & Family

Already within just a few short years after the Internet explosion to the American public, we are seeing multitudes of patients in our offices with sexual addictions and even what some clinicians are referring to as "internet addiction." This phenomenon is not only seen with males, but a significant increased number of women and even adolescents and children are now involved with such addictive behaviors.

Several studies that examine the web sites most frequently visited by individuals clearly without exception report that pornographic sites exceed any other web site in popularity. What has become referred to as "internet affairs" quite often start with individuals "chatting" to someone they meet while surfing on the Internet and visiting various chat rooms. What may seem quite innocent at first will frequently result with the persons agreeing to meet in person; unfortunately many progress quickly to sexual contact, destroying their marriage and devastating their family.

Divorce—Is It Ever Appropriate?

While Jesus was always pro-marriage and anti-divorce throughout his ministry, and divorce is not God's perfect will for anyone, there are some occasions where He permits divorce. Scripturally, it would appear that divorce would be permitted legitimately in only three conditions: adultery or immorality, abuse, and abandonment. Jesus speaks to the issue of adultery in Matthew 19:9, Moses speaks to the issue of abuse as referenced in Matthew 19:8, and finally Paul speaks to the issue of abandonment in I Corinthians 7. Some have adhered to a rather legalistic interpretation of scripture that very narrowly defines biblical grounds while others take such a liberal view that it is not much different than one would find in the secular world. Somewhere in the middle of these two extremes we can find a balance that contains "grace" which Jesus demonstrated throughout His ministry on earth.

Summary

Each of the chapters to follow is devoted to enlarging these twelve critical spiritual issues. While reading this book will not guarantee victory in these areas nor should it take the place of working through such conflicts with a Christian psychologist or counselor, the insights provided here might be helpful in broadening our understanding and help to reduce subtle vulnerability we all face every day.

Chapter 2

Important Boundaries For A Life Of Holiness

Significantly troubled with obvious depressive symptoms, Charles had been referred to me by his pastor. After calling his insurance company and jumping through the various hoops of getting pre-approved for psychotherapeutic services, he had called and made an appointment to see me. As he sat in the waiting room, he appeared in deep thought as if he were contemplating what he would share about his condition. He had chosen to avoid any interaction with other patients and did not try to occupy his time with looking at any of the host of reading materials available. Finally, it was his turn and I greeted him for the first time as I invited him back to my office.

After responding to rather generic questions asked of all new patients in an effort to get helpful information about them while establishing a level of rapport, I asked Charles, "Charles, what brings you in to see me today ... how can I help you with the depression you are experiencing?" Working hard to minimize the appearance of pain on his countenance, he shared for several minutes about his marriage of 17 years to a woman whom he reported had not brought happiness into his life.

"We got married so young and really didn't understand what love is ... we probably should not have ever gotten married at all ... we really are so different…we are just not compatible … " were among the many descriptions he used as he built the background for what he would later share to be the source of his discomfort. He and his wife had three children, aged between 8 and 16 years of age. Although indicating he was somewhat involved in their lives, he admitted his wife did most of the parenting as his job required a shift rotation and changed frequently since he was a firefighter for the city where he resided. When asked specifically if he loved his wife and family, he responded quickly by saying that he loved his kids very much as he attempted to skirt the issue of loving his wife. When brought back to the question of love for his wife, he hesitated as he responded to the question with words that I have heard far too often in cases like these, "Well, sure I love her and I care for her as a person … she's the mother of my children … I love her, I'm just not 'in' love with her … there isn't any spark, the feelings I once had for her left some time ago."

By this time during an initial therapy session, I am beginning to formulate possible hypotheses as to what may be contributing toward the patient's symptoms. Only after I feel there has been sufficient trust built and there appears to be a good level of rapport with the patient would I move to the next level of more serious questions. Feeling we had progressed to this level, I asked a more specific question of Charles, "Have either you or your wife been involved with anyone outside the marriage in either an emotional or sexual manner?" To this question, the look on Charles face revealed guilt to be a factor in his depression as he turned away and began sharing that he had met a co-worker who he had grown attached to emotionally.

In answering my question, Charles cautiously responded, "You see, Dr. Miller, I work with this woman and she had just gone through a terrible divorce and she really needed someone to talk to; I just wanted to be her friend and a support to her." Trying hard to avoid any expression of being judgmental, I asked Charles to continue. He explained, "it started out just talking together and she said I really helped her by listening to her frustrations … then I began sharing some of my situation with her … she was so much more interested in me than my wife is … she really made me feel important." Charles continued to explain his situation in a manner that would rationalize his decision for the affair; as he discussed his reasoning, it became obvious that he was seeking affirmation or permission from me that what he had chosen to do was certainly understandable. Perhaps like many individuals in similar circumstances, Charles didn't feel he could get such understanding and approval from his pastor, so he chose to come to a Christian Psychologist in hopes that I would "understand" and perhaps partially condone his inappropriate decision-making.

Charles must have anticipated my reluctance to give credence to his rationale as he then desperately expressed that he felt this other woman was a "gift from God" and that God knew he was unhappy in his current marriage. He stated, "God wants us to be happy as His children ... I feel He brought this woman into my life that we might minister to each other ... it's like God sent an angel into my life so that I might be fulfilled and experience the happiness that He desires for me." With such explanations as these, it becomes more difficult guarding against a judgmental spirit as I attempt to help guide a patient through a more accurate interpretation of scripture and the ways in which God works within our lives. As I shared that what he was describing as a gift from God was certainly not that—perhaps a gift from Satan in the form of an attractive temptation at a point of weakness in his life, I could tell Charles was becoming more disenchanted with my interpretation of the cause for his depression. I explained that God never uses anything in our lives that would contradict scripture; and, that what he was describing was "adultery" which is clearly defined in scripture as "sin." I tried to help Charles understand that he had fallen to temptation and that this had led him down the destructive path to sin.

In a desperate attempt to still find any justification for his wrong decision, he asked, "What caused me to do such a thing ... was it something in my childhood that may have made me more susceptible to this sort of thing?" I cautiously tried to help him realize that despite all the psychoanalytical literature that would suggest so many things result from things in our childhood, people basically make decisions. For the most part these decisions are not the result of childhood trauma. I gently prodded him to consider that perhaps the boundaries that should have characterized his marriage had broken down and that although his initial intention was quite likely positive and he had never intended for it to lead to an adulterous affair, one thing had led to another and now he was facing the terrible consequences of his decision. I further tried to share with him that despite the choices he had made and the consequences that would need to be faced, God would forgive him of this sin and perhaps his wife and family would do the same—thus helping him re-establish the type of marriage and family life that God desired for Him. Unfortunately, Charles only came a few more sessions prior to discontinuing therapy. He must have come to the conclusion that I would not endorse the sin in his life that was causing his painful depressive symptoms; I assume he started searching for a different therapist that would accept his decisions as normal and thus excuse his sin.

What ever happened to the "boundaries" we used to hear that were expected of Christians? Perhaps the church previously was too rigid and uncompromising about some things. There was a time in our history that holiness churches appeared more exclusionary in their rigid approach to certain personal convictions. There has been a remarkable change in thinking among the holiness movements— quite likely an overdue change that now portrays the church more as a "mission station" where sinners can come and find relief from the confusion and turbulence sin has placed in their lives. Rather than excluding the sinner, an attempt at building a nonjudgmental relationship is fostered where he or she can perhaps find resolution for the sin problem.

Perhaps the church is now conveying a love for the sinner and as such has become more evangelical in its approach, like Christ's example throughout his ministry here on earth. However, it is here that we must be careful to avoid compromising our methods or thinking to a level that conveys acceptance of not only the sinner but also the sin! While accepting and conveying love toward the sinner, Christ never accepted "sin." Sin has always and will always be repulsive to God; sin breaks the fellowship a believer has with God. It will over time break the relationship one has with God; the saints of old use to call this "backsliding."

We currently live in a culture that promotes having no boundaries. The popular notion is that no one should keep you from finding yourself and your ultimate fulfillment in life no matter where that takes you. No one wants any restraints or expectations placed on them. Compliance to standards or norms seem to stifle one's creativity and thus seen as bad for it prevents personal growth and reaching one's highest potential. The concept of "Boundaries" has recently become negative within the world—perhaps even within the church. Although maintaining appropriate boundaries can be a support for the Christian, it appears that for many, the concept has taken on a negative connotation and as such regarded as unnecessary. Perhaps the church where Charles attended should bear some of the responsibility for his failure as he could continue attending church and not feel convicted of his violation of God's law. He had grown comfortable with his false interpretation of scripture and the nature of God.

The concept of "boundary" can be viewed in a variety of ways: inhibitive, voluntary, or protective. Inhibitive boundaries are constraining or rigid restraints, sometimes negative, and often will produce strong emotional feelings such as resentment, anger, or even bitterness. While not all personal convictions are wrong, if one mandates universal compliance, these could be seen as inhibitive boundaries. Voluntary boundaries on the other hand are optional restraints left to one's own discretion; these boundaries are usually self-serving and generally don't place many limitations on one's actions or behavior. Examples of voluntary boundaries might include dieting or physical exercise routines. Protective boundaries are more conducive and are like safety railings on cliffs; such boundaries can give a sense of safety and security, thus lowering the feelings of fear, insecurity, and anxiety. Protective boundaries help to guard us from outside influences that could be harmful.

Could it be that Charles' church had begun avoiding the concept of "boundaries" all together since the pastor desired to avoid the errors of the past when the church promoted boundaries that were in fact inhibitive and quite likely stifled evangelism efforts? But did he go too far? Charles' church was typical of many churches across the nation; the pastor and church leaders were so focused on church growth and remaining "seeker sensitive" that they had allowed the message to be compromised too much in the area of boundaries. Perhaps Charles' pastor had slipped into the "voluntary" thinking about boundaries. As a result of this philosophy, he encouraged people to create their own boundaries— the kind they felt would help them maintain their personal walk with God. Maybe in its attempt to avoid demanding too much for fear of making the gospel message unattractive, Charles' church failed to emphasize the importance of boundary setting in his life.

We need protective boundaries in many areas of our personal lives: professional, familial, technological, personal-marital, and yes, even in our spiritual life. Without appropriate boundaries in our lives, we can easily find ourselves overly exhausted from fatigue as we are trying to respond to needs that exceed our training or competence. As Christians, we can get caught up in our desire to support and minister to others; at times we might over-step our capabilities and thus find ourselves responding to needs which we should be referring to others who are more adequately trained to better handle such needs. Some special needs require specifically trained persons who God can work through to bring about His healing. While our training and experience may have given us a general knowledge in several areas—we must recognize the limitations of our skills and recognize the wisdom of referring to those whom God has called and equipped through specialized training for meeting these special needs. We can't be everything to everybody. Charles had no formal training in counseling or even supportive ministry that his church offered through their Stephen Ministry program. One of Satan's many tactics to discourage us is to allow us to think it is our duty to serve beyond our capacity. After exhaustion and defeat result, he then can convince us to give up as our efforts either lead to failure or seem in vain. The best and most supportive thing Charles could have done for his co-worker was to encourage her to get the appropriate help she needed, helping her access such referral by giving her names of Christian Counselors in the area, offering to have a Stephen Minister from his church speak with her, and assuring her of his and his wife's prayers during this battle in her life.

A second group of important boundaries are those that protect the family or "familial" boundaries. While Christians are to be available to serve others as God has called all Christians to "go and make disciples of all nations," we must recognize the needs of our family and then make those needs a priority. God has commanded us to serve our families first, then others. I Timothy 3:5 exhorts, "If anyone does not know how to manage his own family, how can he take care of God's church?" This verse of scripture applies to pastor and layperson alike.

A husband's first duty is to his wife. The reverse would also be true—a wife's first duty is to her husband. "Husbands love your wives, just as Christ loved the church and gave himself up for her" (Ephesians 5:25). Married couples need to continue to have a romantic life all through the life span in order to keep the romance fresh and alive! Dating takes time and must become an important priority in a couple's schedule. If dates are not scheduled, they quite often won't happen. God has also commanded necessary time be devoted to children. Psalms 127:3 describe our children as " ... a gift from the Lord." Do we take sufficient time to care for this gift the few short years we have to nurture and tenderly help develop the persons they will become?

Family activities with the kids are a must! Parental attendance at school concerts, ball games, piano recitals are absolutely essential to demonstrate our support and validate their efforts. Perhaps it's okay to arrive a few minutes late to a committee meeting or choir practice since you needed to support your son at his little league ball game or your daughter at a school function. Family activities don't have to be expensive trips to Disney World, but rather more practical and creative events like playing a family game, watching a good movie with popcorn, eating out at McDonalds, and a host of other suggestions children will make if only requested of them. Charles likewise failed miserably here; he neglected his obligations to his wife and family to "minister" as he defined it to a co-worker. Had he followed scriptural guidelines for caring for his wife and family, he would not have had time to share so intimately with this co-worker.

Recent technological advances in our society have provided many blessings to our life styles; such advances have certainly streamlined our lives with a multitude of conveniences. Computer technology alone has advanced our knowledge base extensively and in many respects has been good. This technology can be extremely useful or on the other hand quite destructive. Pastors can now quickly consider various translations of scripture and access a variety of commentaries with the click of the mouse or pressing one key on the keyboard as compared to the multitude of hours such research use to take. A vast wealth of knowledge has been made conveniently accessible to everyone in the household. From searching for information to include in a school project for one of the children to answering questions about side effects for a specific medication that has been prescribed to a family member, computers and the Internet have made this information readily available to everyone.

As a Psychologist, I can now score and interpret a personality profile within a few minutes. Years ago it would take hours to consider only a fraction of the same data. Medical science has been advanced extensively through application of this new technology. Among the number of positive uses, it has facilitated the support system and on-going contact with missionaries and their families, thus enabling more successful terms for missionaries in a foreign land.

It is not the good uses of technology where boundaries are needed for the Christian—but absolute boundaries have become necessary without question for the application it has taken in the secular world and media. The pornographic industry has virtually exploded through the computer Internet. Whereas an individual previously had to go to the adult bookstore to purchase or view such offensive material, now it's available to anyone in the privacy of his or her own home without anyone else knowing. The fear of being seen coming out of an adult bookstore helped deter some men from yielding to temptation for pornography. Now with the Internet, this inhibition is gone; as a result, Satan's efforts at tempting both men and women in this area have increased extensively.

Already within just a few short years after the Internet explosion to the American public, we are seeing multitudes of patients in our offices with sexual addictions and even what some clinicians are referring to "internet addiction". This phenomenon is not only seen with males, but a significant increased number of women and even adolescents and children are now involved with such addictive behaviors. There are now several studies available on the internet usage broken down by age groups; the increasing numbers of hours spent by children and adolescents on the internet is alarming. Is it any wonder that addictive behaviors with this media are so common?

Several studies that examine the web sites most frequently visited by individuals clearly without exception report that pornographic sites exceed any other web site in popularity. What has become referred to as "internet affairs" quite often start with individuals "chatting" to someone they meet while surfing on the Internet and visiting various chat rooms. What may seem quite innocent at first will frequently result with the persons agreeing to meet in person; unfortunately many progress quickly to sexual contact.

After realizing they have destroyed their marriage and family life, some seek therapy and find themselves in our offices. Those of us attempting to treat such problems are appalled to discover that such individuals are among the most educated and sophisticated people in society. Many attend church every Sunday and are actively engaged in their church ministries. No one seems exempt from the potential destruction that pornography can have in his or her life. The absence of boundaries in this area usually results in devastation of one's life and family.

So does this mean that Christians should not utilize the Internet? No, absolutely not; with proper use it can be an extremely useful tool in getting the gospel message out to the world. However, safeguards and boundaries are a must! Careful selection of a server to host your Internet connection that "filters" or protects you from access to pornographic sites should be a definite standard for the Christian. Here again, Charles compromised the appropriate boundaries surrounding the use of his computer. By utilizing computer technology, he could be more available to his co-worker for "chats" on the Instant Messaging Service. Since Charles made more use of the Internet for their secret communications, the temptation to explore the various pornographic e-mails and related websites that came unsolicited became more of a problem for him.

Protective boundaries that guard one's personal devotional life are necessary to preserve the time set aside to cultivate one's own spiritual life which then prepares them for ministry to others— whether clergy or lay person. Everyone must have a consistent devotional and prayer life; we can't rely totally on the church for our spiritual nurturing. Church life should be seen as a supplement and validation of the personal walk one has with God. To avoid becoming "weary in well doing" we must take time to nourish our own souls prior to ministering to others. It is so easy to become so task oriented in fulfilling the demands of our various roles that devotions are neglected due to insufficient time allotted in our schedules.

I encourage my patients to establish a regular, daily devotional time that occurs on a consistent basis. I would rather see a shorter time each day that is a consistent part of the schedule rather than trying to have a "marathon" ever so often to catch up. Of course, in order to accomplish this goal, time management is helpful; self-discipline is an absolute must! In addition to regular services provided by one's church, participating in retreats, camp meetings, and neighboring church revivals can supplement the spiritual nurturing provided to one's spiritual diet. Such supplemental activities can enhance one's depth of spirituality; and thus, better prepare them for the tasks in their daily schedule. Due to the distractions in his life, Charles had discontinued his personal devotional life that had previously been a more regular part of his daily schedule. He rationalized this on the basis that he was devoting his time to serving others and didn't have time to do both.

As professional, familial, and technological boundaries deteriorated, less and less time were allotted to the important functions in his life and family; this process seemed to progressively lead to the elimination of perhaps the most important boundary in Charles' life—personal and marital. Violation of this boundary can and very often will lead to an adulterous affair just as it did with Charles.

From my perspective as a psychologist, perhaps the most important boundary seen violated or neglected in today's world has to do with personal-marital issues. Of the various compromises Charles made, this one was the most significant and swiftly led to his decision for sin! While we are called to minister to a dying world, we must recognize the ultimate need to remain faithful to our spouses in all ways—not just sexually, but emotionally as well! Perhaps a sad commentary, violation of this boundary is in crisis proportions within the general public—and such a phenomenon would quite likely also characterize the church as well. Unfortunately, Charles probably represents multitudes of examples one would find within churches across the nation.

In recent discussions with church leaders, I have shared recent trends in my own practice that very much distress me as a Christian Psychologist. Only a few short years ago, patients presenting with symptoms as the result of adultery in their lives might occur 6 or 7 times a year at most. Now, sad to say, at least 1 or 2 and sometimes 3 cases are seen on a weekly basis. My patients presenting with these problems or other problems resulting from the adultery are for the most part from evangelical and quite often holiness churches. The vast majority claim to know Christ and report being saved; some even claim holiness of heart!

Dr. Keith Drury, an ordained minister, published author, and leader within the Wesleyan Church, has studied and written about the issue of adultery extensively. Based on sixty letters from individuals attending holiness churches that had fallen to an adulterous affair, Dr. Drury constructed what he conceptualized as a 15-step process (1) that could surely lead one to unfaithfulness with their marriage. As I considered the case of my patient—Charles, I could easily see the progression of these steps and how they progressively led him to the devastating place he now found himself. Let's examine the steps Dr. Drury proposed and correlate them with Charles' dilemma:

1. **Sharing common interests:** Charles told me that he and his co-worker were both firefighters and they shared common interests. He rationalized that his wife wasn't interested in the same hobbies and that they had very little in common other than their children. As

he began sharing with his friend on a personal level, an important boundary was violated. Such personal sharing should be reserved for one's spouse. If interests and hobbies are different, then new ones need to be explored to gain some common ground. One's spouse must be one's best friend in a good marriage!

2. **Mentally comparing with mate:** Charles began comparing this co-worker's attributes with those of his wife; this led to further evaluation of skills, hobbies, and interests. His co-worker appeared more "in shape" and slimmer than his wife since she got regular physical exercise on her job. As his thinking continued to progress it led to dangerous fantasizing. Scripture (Philippians 4:8) suggests that one should think about virtuous things and warns us against such fantasizing!

3. **Meeting emotional needs:** Charles conveyed to me that his co-worker certainly seemed to understand him better than his own wife; she likewise had told him that he had such insight into her feelings and further affirmed him by telling him he was a "good listener" and how that really helped her feel better. In what could be considered the beginning stages of rationalization, Charles shared, "But she understands me and allows me to affirm her ... my wife doesn't ... how could this be wrong when it makes me so happy?" People can rationalize almost anything; after a while, they begin to believe as "rational" what previously would have been considered "irrational." Perhaps this very process of rationalizing behaviors led Charles to the irrational conclusion that God had brought this woman into his life as a "gift" to provide him with happiness.

4. **Looking forward to being together:** Charles' job became more rewarding than it had been before since he began looking forward to spending more time with this co-worker. If projects around the station required more than one worker, he would often

volunteer the two of them to complete the task as they could "legitimately" spend more focused time together. This of course provided more time to share at personal levels and become more acquainted with each other's lives.

5. **Tinges of dishonesty with mate:** Charles began to justify spending more time on his job than he previously had done; he also began to convey to other workers at his station that he really didn't mind picking up the extra hours or tasks, carefully minimizing or ignoring the rather obvious observations that such times would usually be when his female friend was also on duty. In discussing with Charles' wife in later sessions, she shared that she initially thought her husband began working more hours to demonstrate a deeper commitment or dedication to his job. She further explained, "He always seemed to have legitimate reasons for working extra hours or needing to attend a special meeting ... whenever I asked him about things, he never hesitated in explaining the purpose of his involvement ... he even told me he would like to be considered for a supervisory level position and thought his extra efforts would pave the way for such an opportunity in the future." From a psychologist's perspective, healthy marriages have no secrets! Secrets are toxic and Satan can utilize such matters to tempt, discourage, and eventually erode the marriage—just as he had done in Charles' case.

6. **Flirting and teasing:** Perhaps starting out innocently, things progress to gestures of flirtation, joking with each other, and even some teasing that can be interpreted by the recipient as somewhat romantic or sexual in nature. Charles shared that he really enjoyed the way his co-worker laughed at his jokes; he also added that she was fun to tease. He again rationalized that his wife didn't laugh much and always seemed too busy with the children or household duties that she

had become boring to him. He conveyed, "My friend is like a breath of fresh air in smog." He further admitted that the more they talked to each other; the positive feelings for each other began to grow. This process is subtle, but powerful; sin usually seems so innocent in the beginning, but it will take one much further than he or she ever thought was possible. While it will ultimately lead to destruction of those most important things and relationships in one's life, this process builds with an excitement and energy of its own—it seems to blind one from seeing clearly the potential destruction to which it leads!

7. **Talking about personal matters:** Too many affairs have started when one decided, out of Christian love, to try to be someone's "friend" or "minister to someone in need." Many affairs could be avoided entirely if rather than trying to be a personal confidante; he or she merely referred that person to a reputable Christian therapist. Charles utilized most of the excuses I've heard multiple times, "I was just trying to be her friend … she needed someone to talk to and had no one … I was just trying to be a Christian brother to her … I saw her as a needy person that I needed to help as a Christian who is concerned about other people … What was I to do? … I couldn't just desert her!" Charles had started listening to his co-worker's problems; conversations lengthened and began to include more reciprocal sharing with her about his personal life, which only served to deepen the relationship between the two of them.

8. **Minor yet arousing touch, squeeze, or hug:** Charles confessed that shortly into the process of sharing with each other, he "felt led to just give her a hug since she was feeling so lonely and probably hadn't been hugged by anyone for some time." He rationalized that he was sure it didn't convey any kind of affection but merely that he understood her and wanted her to feel

cared about by someone. Of course, you can guess that the hugs became more regular and elongated as discussions became more frequent and on deeper matters; it was soon very difficult for Charles to rationalize the innocent intent of his concluding hug after their discussions. As we discussed his problem in psychotherapy, Charles admitted that he realized now that the hugs had taken on more meaning—almost a secret or romantic meaning. He likewise admitted to other subtle touches as they passed each other in the station; he agreed that these too had become more frequent and obviously had taken on the same deeper meaning to the both of them. Although touching can be therapeutic, it can also be a set-up for misinterpretation. As a psychologist and marriage therapist, I don't give therapeutic hugs to my patients! Boundaries are an important thing I model for my patients! My hugs are appropriately reserved for my wife and family.

9. **Special notes or gifts:** Charles shared that he would at times leave "a note of encouragement" on his co-worker's desk or in the pocket of her jacket. Like many who fall into the rationalization trap, Charles tried to convince himself that these activities were just another visible way that would demonstrate his innocent support for her. Charles reported that he actually felt proud of his creativity in designing ways to encourage her through notes, facial expressions, gestures, or even an occasional gift of something he had learned that she cherished. Due to their jobs, both Charles and his co-worker were required to carry pagers and cell phones; this provided more opportunities for "expressions of encouragement" that became more frequent and more personal in nature to the degree that they both agreed to change their password codes so Charles' wife could not access any of her messages to him.

10. **Inventing excuses to call or meet:** The more involved this relationship became, the more Charles or his co-worker desired to have contact. He reluctantly agreed with me as I pointed out that some of the reasons he used for the two of them to meet were merely excuses to have more time together and not really required for their job. As a Psychologist, I know that people have the capacity to develop a very sophisticated defense system to protect their ego. Charles had fallen into this trap; he had become quite skilled in rationalizing his behaviors. People can rationalize and justify just about anything these days!

11. **Arranging secret meetings:** Charles admitted they started meeting secretly since the legitimate meeting times didn't seem enough for either of them after a few weeks. He agreed to walk her to the parking lot or even follow her home at times; Charles rationalized to himself that this was done so that she "might feel safer and more secure." Within a short time, they began stopping after work for coffee or a sandwich together—rationalized by Charles as "merely a business type lunch with a co-worker."

12. **Deceit and cover-ups:** As the meeting times became more frequent and taking a larger amount of personal time away from his family, Charles shared he was forced to tell his wife some "white lies." He rationalized that he wasn't outright lying to her, but only hiding some minor things to protect her; if she found out she would no doubt "become angry, stressed, and even might suspect something that wasn't happening … " Charles shared that he even discussed this concern with his co-worker, and the two of them strategized together the explanations to use when questioned by his wife or others. You remember they had already changed their password codes to cell phones to prevent Charles' wife from getting their messages to each other. I didn't bother to ask Charles

what reason he gave his wife when she asked why he had changed the code and had his cell phone bill sent to the station rather than the home address.

13. **Kissing and embracing**
14. **Petting and high indiscretion**
15. **Sexual intercourse:** Charles admitted that by the time he and his co-worker had progressed to step 12, they moved quite swiftly through the latter three steps. Like most patients who are being treated for depression following adultery, Charles conveyed that he seriously never thought it would have ever led to this decision. He was adamant that his initial intent was merely to help a person in distress; he reasoned, "I'm just not sure how it progressed to this point ... it feels so good at times ... but at other times I really feel guilty ... how could something be wrong if it brings so much happiness ... it's like we just couldn't help ourselves—we couldn't prevent the natural urges we both had for each other ... we just couldn't stop ourselves ... we finally gave in to our strong feelings for each other!" Actually steps 11-14 generally progress rather rapidly in the affair— almost like the momentum has taken over without any regard for reason or rational thinking. At this stage in the process, there is usually a feeling of having gone too far to return; thus Satan's grip on one's life has been strengthened and usually leads to the 15th step.

When sharing this information with couples in a marriage retreat or in a therapy session as with the case of Charles, I ask at what step in this process, does "adultery" become a reality. As you might suspect, I get a variety of answers—the majority of which are much later in the sequence (steps 13—15) since it is at that point that "touching" starts. However, doesn't scripture (Matthew 5:28) reference such thinking and fantasizing, even when it is merely conceived in the mind, as committing adultery in the heart? If this is the case, then doesn't "adultery" start back in the beginning steps? As with many, this was not a popular notion with Charles. Although I assured him that therapy and anti-depressant medications could help reduce the symptoms he was experiencing, the causal factor was actually a spiritual one and would require a spiritual healing to eliminate the root cause of his depression. When he could see that I would not excuse the effect that this sin had taken in his life, he discontinued therapy.

Appropriate boundaries in the life of a Christian are essential! While avoiding an emphasis on the inhibitive and voluntary boundaries, perhaps the church could promote the importance of "protective" boundaries. It is protective boundaries that protect us from falling into the multiple traps set by the enemy; and permits us to experience a freedom in Christ that should characterize a life of holiness. Should we not return to a time of promoting such boundaries as both essential and necessary in our Christian walk? Perhaps taking a "balanced" approach to boundary setting and focusing on the protective nature that such boundaries can provide for the Christian, will support our efforts at living a life of holiness within a world that is unholy.

Chapter 3

Anger—Is It Wrong?

Julie was a 43-year-old single female who presented with a multitude of symptoms ranging from clinical depression and generalized anxiety to a deep-seated bitterness caused from anger over a very traumatic event that had occurred in her life 23 years before. Julie was the victim of one of the worst cases of rape that I have seen in over 20 years of practice. As a young lady in her 20's, she had befriended a man while a student at Kent State University, started dating him only to learn after several weeks that he was a married man with a family. Upon discovering this news, which he had kept from her initially, she had broken off the relationship indicating that she was not interested in further dates since he was married. Thinking this was the right thing to do, she encouraged him to go back to his wife and family; she thought she would move on and continue her search for a single man who could fulfill her dream of marriage and raising a family together. Although somewhat older than Julie, she had fallen for this man initially since he pursued her, complimented her, and made her feel important after having grown up in a home of neglect, abuse, and parenting techniques that minimized her importance as a person. This man could easily get Julie's attention as she had entered into this stage of her life with a host of unmet affirmation needs. She was starved for attention; she quickly had fallen into what she felt were the beginning stages of love, hoping he would eventually marry her and provide her the safe home of love and affection that had not characterized the home where she had grown up.

On the evening of that day when she had confidently informed this man she could no longer see him, Julie got off work at the usual time only to discover that this man was in the parking lot where he forced her to get into his car. Since fear and anxiety overwhelmed her, she helplessly complied. He then proceeded to drive several blocks in route to a destination of which Julie was not familiar. Her fear began to deepen as she observed a side of this man she had not seen before; the cold, calculating expression on his face triggered memories of the times her mother and father had abused her as a child. She quickly tried to open her door only to discover the handle had been removed and thus she had no way of escaping; she thought for a moment and begged the man to stop at a gasoline station as she convinced him she had to use the bathroom. After some hesitation, he pulled into a station, found the outside bathroom where he parked the car in a manner that would easily facilitate her capture by him should she decide to try escaping. Opening the door from the outside, he let her use the bathroom while waiting at the car for her return. Although franticly thinking through various plans of escape, Julie decided she could not successfully accomplish this goal and sheepishly opened the bathroom door where he met her to escort her back to his automobile. Once she was back in the passenger's side, he quickly jumped in the driver's side and resumed the same unfamiliar route they had started several blocks before.

After several more blocks, he turned down a road that appeared as if they were leaving the residential population of homes they had followed; suddenly, he turned into a cemetery and proceeded back into the heart of the graveyard safely away from any of the roads leading to this place. Now forcing her out of the car, he ripped her clothing from her and viciously raped her on the ground in front of several tombstones. After what seemed to be hours to Julie, she was forcibly placed back into his car and taken back to her apartment where he dropped her off and then quickly drove off, leaving her standing on the curb in front of her apartment complex. Bleeding excessively and in physical pain worse than she had ever experienced in her 20 years of life, she slowly made her way up the sidewalk and steps leading to her apartment. After letting herself in, she dropped onto her bed where she would remain for the next several hours. It was two or three days later that Julie finally cleaned herself up and dressed her wounds as best she could; although feeling she should go to the hospital or a physician, she feared the consequences of such a decision and this fear rendered her powerless to seek appropriate medical attention. She was both embarrassed and fearful, but the fear is what immobilized her over the days and weeks to follow. She was extremely fearful that she might be sought again by this man; but more than that she feared that if she went for help, she would be blamed for this act of violence—just like her mother had done when abusing her throughout her childhood. At times she would blame herself for having even been willing to date this man; she assumed he would rationalize his conduct—just like her father use to do after sexually abusing her in the incestuous home environment of which she was raised.

After a few weeks of solitude, Julie decided to leave college and her apartment in an attempt to put this terrible memory out of her mind. Thinking that by starting a new life, living in a different geographical location and starting a different job, she might be able to begin sleeping at night and perhaps the terrible nightmares that haunted her would eventually leave and some form of peace and safety would return to her world. After weeks of sleepless nights, panic attacks, and dealing with the deep depressive and anxiety symptoms that characterized each of her days resulting from that tragic night in the cemetery, Julie's emotions began to stabilize until they were shattered once again when discovering she was pregnant as a result of this rape. Although in desperation she considered abortion for a moment, Julie could not bring herself to choose such an option and decided to carry the baby to term. As you might expect, she chose never to inform her son's father of his fatherhood or attempt getting any help or support for this child for she feared he would kill them both to protect his reputation since he was a well-known architect that had built several of the buildings at the university where she had attended.

Now, 23 years later, Julie had made her way to my clinical office and expressed a desire to address the deep seated feelings of anger, hostility, bitterness, and hate that had characterized her life over the previous 23 years as she was reminded daily of the trauma that had occurred on the night at the cemetery. Sitting in my waiting room, her body language revealed a sense of desperation; her facial expression was bland, without any recognizable expression of affect. Upon being greeted and invited to join me in my office for an initial evaluative session, she complied, forcing the artificial smile that had been well rehearsed for much of her life. Although quickly responding to my invitation, she exhibited no optimism or sense of hope that this activity would help to ease her pain in any way. Julie had tried therapy several times before this occasion; she had never gotten beyond the extremely bitter hatred that had come to characterize her total life—affecting all aspects of her life including her job, neighborhood, family, and the very few friendships she developed. She struggled especially in her relationships with men. She was thus somewhat overwhelmed in rearing a son who through no fault of his own had served to remind her daily of the man who had victimized her the worst on that tragic night in the cemetery. Even though she had remembered her mother scalding her as an infant and subsequently attempting to drown her during a bath at age four, abuse at the hands of the males in her life had left her with the deepest scars.

She had quit or been terminated from several jobs due to her uncontrollable anger. Although trying to find a church, she typically only stayed a short time, as she would become so uncomfortable in that setting she would leave to escape the inner pain of feeling rejected. She described what she felt had become a predictable pattern with her involvement in churches or other religious organizations; she would frequently get her feelings hurt and feel further victimized by others, which usually caused her to swiftly escape as a means of avoiding further pain. She admitted that on other occasions, she knew something would trigger conflict in her and she would lose control of the unresolved anger that totally controlled her life. On these occasions, she felt compelled to leave, as she didn't feel supported by others in the fellowship and knew her relentless and vicious attacks in retaliation only caused them to experience similar pain. She admitted feeling justified at times, as she wanted others to experience the deep pangs of inner turmoil that had characterized her life for so many years. Julie shared with me on that first day that she knew she needed to work in therapy with a male therapist, but at the same time questioned if she could trust me—after all, she had not been able to trust the other males in her life. Though doubtful of her capacity to trust, she committed to try since she desired more than anything else to reach the healing she desperately needed.

I must confess that I felt literally unprepared, and certainly inadequate to handle such a case as Julie's. I remember sharing with her on that first day of her treatment that I possessed no supernatural skills or powers; but, that if she would learn to trust me and allow God to work in her life—I was confident that she could conquer what had kept her captive for these last 23 years. As I shared how only God could bring about the healing she so desperately needed, she listened intently, but with much doubt as she had heard this line several times before even by those whom she felt had subsequently hurt her. She confessed she didn't even feel she could trust God; after all, "where was He when I needed protected from my mother's wrath and my father's perversion ... where was He when that man raped me ... where has He been on those lonely, dark nights that I have had no where to turn?" Julie further explained her disbelief that even God really understood her pain as she shared what she termed as her deepest loss. She said that just a few years before, she had met a man who appeared to genuinely love her; they had fallen in love, became engaged to be married, but just days before the wedding he died suddenly of a massive heart attack. She explained that "this God you're trying to tell me loves and cares for me took the only man I have ever been able to trust."

Why was Julie experiencing such intense levels of anger? Why had her anger rendered her powerless and defeated over so many years? Was her anger legitimate? Was it wrong? Was her anger sinful or a form of righteous indignation? Is this level of anger a sign of carnality or inbred sin? These are examples of the multitude of questions that people like Julie represent. To minister to persons like Julie, we must gain insight into the emotion of anger; wisdom for helping such a person understand the causal factors of his or her anger, and ultimately how to resolve such issues in a healthy manner—thus allowing them to once and for all gain victory over it and find the peace and tranquility that only such inner-healing can provide.

Psychologists describe anger as an emotion; like love, joy, happiness, it is an emotional response to some stimulus. "Along with joy, surprise, fear, disgust, and distress or sadness, anger has been seen as a primary human emotion that has evolved to enhance the adaptation and survival of the species" (Lemerise & Dodge, 1993). (1) Anger, in and of itself, is not wrong! Emotions are not wrong; nor are they sin! Webster (1996) defines anger as "a strong feeling of displeasure aroused by a real or supposed wrong." (2) Webster goes on to further differentiate levels of anger by comparing **indignation, rage, and fury. Indignation** is usually seen as a more formal response to something people feel is wrong; it implies what Webster (1996) would describe as a "justified anger, often directed at something unworthy." (3) Indignation usually results when a scandal is made public; the public is outraged with the immoral or ethical compromises that are exposed. Webster described **rage** as "a vehement, uncontrolled anger." (4) Rage often results when one has lost something for which they feel they are entitled; rage may or may not be legitimate, but at any rate it is a strong emotional response that seemingly lacks the control seen with indignation. According to Webster, **fury** is "rage so great it resembles insanity" (5); fury is the uncontrollable anger that usually results in aggressive attacks on others and is represented as the causal factor of physical assaults on others or even murder.

Scripture also gives insight into the emotion of anger. First of all, Ephesians 4:26-7 clearly gives us permission to become angry for anger is not sin, "In your anger do not sin … " Christ Himself became angry when He saw injustices. In response to the Pharisees accusing Him of healing on the Sabbath, "He (Christ) looked around at them in anger and, [became] deeply distressed at their stubborn hearts … " (Mark 3:5). Then there is a favorite example of Christ displaying anger in John 2:14-16 when finding men in the temple area selling cattle, sheep and doves while others were exchanging money at tables. Scripture documents appropriate anger in that He (Christ) " ... made a whip out of cords, and drove all from the temple area, both sheep and cattle; he scattered the coins of the money changers and overturned their tables ... he said, Get these out of here ... How dare you turn my Father's house into a market!" This is an excellent example of **indignation,** which is described above. Many in Christian circles refer to this anger as **"righteous indignation"** and justify it as legitimate or appropriate. My personal rendition of the temple scene also includes Christ throwing a couple of chairs against the wall to get their attention—then he drives them out of the courts and warns them about the appropriate use of His Father's House. Whether or not chairs were thrown, the scene is clearly a display of appropriate anger for legitimate causes; since Christ did not sin, such a display for the same purpose is also not sin for mankind.

On the other hand, anger can become sin if it leads to what scripture describes as bitterness. This form of anger would be better described as rage and fury, thus leading to the expression of uncontrollable aggressive acts and can progress to irrational acts in retaliation and a personal vengeance. We are warned about this kind of anger in Colossians 3:8, " ... you must rid yourselves of all such things as these: anger, rage, malice, slander, and filthy language from your lips." Further described in scripture as a "form of malice," this anger is anything but legitimate and rapidly becomes sin. Scripture further commands "Get rid of all bitterness, rage and anger, brawling and slander, along with every form of malice" (Ephesians 4:31).

Perhaps another way of understanding anger is to see it as an emotion or attribute that God's creation provided us. When expressed in an appropriate manner and with a pure heart for legitimate or valid causes, it is healthy anger—and not sin! If this God-given attribute becomes perverted in some way, then it can swiftly lead to bitterness or carnal anger, which is sin. "Carnality is merely a perversion of any God-given attribute" (Hotle, 1999). (6)

In the case of my patient—Julie, her anger initially started out as legitimate anger—indignation. What had happened to her was absolutely wrong; the abuse from both her parents and the man who raped her as a young lady could never be rationalized in any way!

Her strong response to this devastation to her life and body was most appropriate; however, in the absence of resolution it grew into bitterness that progressed to the formation of a bitter hatred and distrust for all men. It interfered with her ability to form relationships with others, especially men. It destroyed her belief in male pastors or therapists who may have been able to minister to her needs. It led her to form the irrational conclusion that she could not trust God. Distancing herself from others, she became further depressed and alienated from the very people who may have been capable of helping her heal. Typical of persons with anger problems, Julie became rigid, legalistic, and inflexible in her belief system. She often utilized anger as a defense mechanism to protect her from painful truths or feelings about herself. Also quite common, she exhibited other emotional symptoms that are commonly associated with angry persons; these include fear, stress, tension, and worry. Julie also admitted to having feelings of insecurity, inadequacy, and her whole demeanor dramatically reflected her extremely low self-esteem, which made her quite vulnerable to getting hurt. Such persons often complain of feeling fatigue; if honest, most will admit to a general predisposition to irritability. Like a majority of severely depressed persons as a result of such trauma in their life, Julie exemplified extreme anger or rage since this was easier to handle than to admit the severe pain that she experienced from the deep hurt and scars that she carried.

Although more commonly seen in men than women who experience depression, Julie seemed to find it easier to admit to struggling with unmanageable anger as opposed to expressing the deep hurt and sadness. Psychologists find in working with such people that it may be easier for them to be angry (mad) than to identify and admit depression (sad). Furthermore, anger is usually very much associated to depression; depression can be merely a suppressed anger or what some would term "anger turned inward." We find depression is often the presenting symptom of a patient who feels the expression or even identification of anger within them is wrong. Therefore, it seems better to them to feel depressed rather than take the chance of being displeasing to God since it is their perception that anger is sin.

Still others would perceive the admission of depression or sadness to be a sign of weakness, therefore their emotions are externalized through anger. Such outbursts or attacks on others serve to protect them from any further hurt they fear might result in trusting others. By alienating others and displacing such anger onto them, one's ability to interpret interactions and the motives of others objectively is severely damaged. Within time, such a person concludes they can trust no one and they must always be on the defensive, thus guarding against the next abuse they predict will occur. Like Julie, they adopt a philosophy that promotes "attack first ... to avoid being attacked."

Although at times internalizing the pain so severely that she contemplated taking her own life, Julie shared that she could never follow through with such thoughts of suicide as she feared to do so would cause her son, now 23 years of age, to experience similar severe pain that she had sustained over the larger part of her life. Perhaps for this reason, Julie's depression mostly took the form of a bitter anger, thus helping her to keep hidden the overwhelming sadness that predominated her life.

Julie's course of treatment lasted for several months and finally concluded successfully after about 2 years. The only goal for early sessions centered on helping her reach an ability "to trust" by working through the extremely well defended boundaries that she had created over the years to protect her from further pain. Once sufficient trust was established, efforts transitioned to helping Julie work through the painful memories and begin to reach resolution of these traumas in her life. Typical of victims with such deep trauma, the course of therapy seemed rocky and discouraging; she would make good progress and begin feeling optimistic about recovery, then relapse by slipping back into an old coping pattern or way of thinking. Julie's thinking and ways of reacting with hostility and anger or bitterness were habitual in nature; she had developed these patterns over 23 years and to break such habits and replace them with other more appropriate coping behaviors and thinking was not an easy process.

For several weeks, Julie was asked to share the details of her traumatic life, beginning with the childhood victimization that no doubt made her more vulnerable to the victimization that characterized her adulthood. Detail after detail was shared painfully as Julie forced herself to remember things she had tried to forget. After sharing events of her childhood trauma, she then moved to the rape and subsequent abuses and hurts that characterized her adult life. In sharing even with me as her psychologist, someone whom she had begun to trust, she was often quite troubled and distressed by uncovering these deeply buried memories. Rather than feeling a catharsis of relief, such times resulted in Julie crying and at times weeping, almost hysterically. On some occasions, usually in addressing the very deepest wounds, Julie would spontaneously develop a nosebleed. She likewise began experiencing severe physical pain in her back and abdominal regions; this pain is known as psychogenic or psychosomatic in nature since it is real pain but has no medical basis, but caused by the mind.

In Julie's case, sharing these things in therapy prompted "trigger memories" so her physical body re-experienced the same pain she had experienced that night of the rape where she had sustained significant internal injury. Now, 23 years later, other than scar tissue from the initial injuries, there was no physiological cause for the pain that she experienced. By forcing her mind to remember these events, the memory of the pain she sustained at the time of injury was thus re-experienced—much like a flashback. Once explained to her that this was a common occurrence when healing from such trauma, the pain mysteriously dissipated after about 2 weeks. But despite these inconveniences and at times feeling worse than before treatment, Julie persevered in sharing what was asked of her; she was determined to gain resolution and freedom from the hurt and pain that had characterized the majority of her adult life. After giving the last detail, she was irritated and confused when I asked her to begin once again from the beginning as I wished for her to share her story a second time. She begged to differ, claiming that she had already shared everything and she couldn't bear the thought of re-experiencing the pain she had felt when telling her story the first time.

This process of externalizing the repressed anger through "telling one's story" is a common technique utilized in treatment with victims of severe trauma. Some of the very first psychiatrists and psychologists utilized this technique in what was known in those days as psychoanalysis. By allowing someone else to hear about her secret, both clarification of issues and validation of her pain were made possible. While the first time of sharing for Julie was literally almost like re-experiencing the trauma, the second and third times helped her reach a more objective frame of reference, thereby placing it in her past, rather than present. The subsequent times of sharing her story were less emotional; it was almost like she was telling a story about someone else rather than herself. By considering it more objectively, she was then more open and prepared to consider the dynamics and issues rather than remain overwhelmed with the anger that had become her safety net against further hurt or abuse.

While this story telling technique is not recommended for an untrained person and should only be utilized with a trained clinician who can help guide the process, there were several other practical things that Julie was asked to do while in therapy that played a role in the victory she would eventually achieve. She became a student of anger; she began reading everything she could read about the subject matter that had been written from a spiritual frame of reference. Knowledge is very powerful; the more understanding she gained about this emotion and how it manifests itself within man, the easier it was for her to consider the unresolved conflicts that it had caused in her life. She gathered books, videos, pamphlets, and various articles she could find addressing this issue. She wrote letters to the various individuals that had victimized her—letters that were not to be sent—but only done in the process of therapy, thus helping her gain a sense of relief for having expressed her strong emotions to the source of the conflict. She made a couple of trips back to the graveyard where she was raped; these trips helped her overcome the "powerlessness" that had governed her and prevented her from forming relationships with others for fear they too would result in victimization.

Although listening to many sermons and reading a multitude of written materials on this subject, Julie found the most practical for her to be a sermon preached by Dr. Thomas Hermiz at Mt. Of Praise Camp Meeting in1997 entitled "Get Rid Of All Bitterness." It was this sermon that seemed to help Julie outline the following four simple steps to eliminate the bitterness that had overtaken her whole being: (7)

(1)   Julie had to **begin acknowledging the fact that she had become bitter;** her initial anger which was caused by legitimate hurts, abuse, rejection or other deep hurts, had progressed to bitterness

(2)   Through prayerful guidance, she came to **recognize her bitterness as sin and displeasing to God;** with much encouragement she confessed and surrendered it to God

(3)   Though much more difficult than the first two steps, Julie had to **become willing to forgive the people who had hurt or wronged her in any way**

(4)   Finally, Julie then had to **commit to stop remembering the details or dwelling on these past hurts;** she had to "let it go" and **force her mind to think on other things**—perhaps more pleasant memories

It is very interesting that as Julie began working through these steps, she was able to begin remembering some pleasant memories of her childhood that she had long forgotten as they seemed to be overshadowed by the hurts that had predominated her thinking. In essence, she began the process of "renewing her mind" and directing it away from the things that caused her pain.

Julie began listing the people she had refused to forgive and the multitude of offenses they represented. One by one, each situation and individual was processed in therapy sessions in an effort to better understand how someone could have hurt her so deeply and move toward the goal of forgiveness in an effort to reach resolution. Some were easier than others and this step in the process literally endured for many hours over several weeks, but finally this step in her recovery had been completed. Each offense and offender had been listed, discussed for clarification of the event or issue, and then processed extensively in therapy.

When Julie was satisfied that she had given enough explanation to each item on her list which included several pages, we had discussed having a "burning ceremony" to symbolically signify she was once and for all giving these items over to God. You see, Julie had for many years tried to administer justice and punish her offenders. She finally came to realize that her anger was wrathful, vengeful and resembled fury; her bitterness had produced a rage within her that was quickened by her against anyone from whom she felt threatened. After reviewing Romans 12:17-19 which admonishes, "Do not repay anyone evil for evil ... be careful to do what is right in the eyes of everybody ... do not take revenge, my friends, but leave room for God's wrath, for it is written: It is mine to avenge, says the Lord," the ceremony was scheduled. Carefully placing the lists within a bucket and after prayer requesting God's blessing and favor on this step in Julie's process of treatment, the papers were set on fire with a match. Julie and I watched the fire literally consume the multitude of offenses documented on those pieces of paper. As Julie patiently watched the record of what represented years of agony and deep emotional hurt change to ashes, her countenance changed! "Dr. Miller, I really did forgive them ... I felt God touch me ... He did something as I watched the fire consume my record of their wrongs ... I truly do forgive them!"

Further sessions were scheduled, but with a new focus—learning how to live victoriously despite the potential hurts and disappointments that might come her way. Now utilizing as her motto, " ... I do not consider myself yet to have taken hold of it; but one thing I do, forgetting what is behind and straining toward what is ahead, I press on toward the goal to win the prize for which God has called me heavenward in Christ Jesus"(Philippians 3:13-14). Julie realized that she might be troubled from time to time with a memory of these past traumas, but by adhering to this motto, she had the strength to seek God's grace and could overcome those times of discouragement, refusing to return to the past misery she had overcome. She later told me that she had carried the bottle of ashes in her purse for months as a visual cue of the choice she had made at the burning ceremony to forgive and resolve.

This chapter is concluded with Julie's own account of her story which is used with her permission: (8)

My heart pounding through my chest as though it were a high powered pressure hammer pounding out steel, destroying its own encasement. Exhaustion as that of one who has wandered aimlessly and alone for a thousand years carrying the weight of a hundred cities on their shoulders. In my mind I have slayed so many dragons my sword never stops flailing. Blinded by the darkness and tossed about by the winds I struggle through life without direction or foundation. Once I walked mightily, believing God was on my side, destroying doctors' predictions and making folly of the doom and gloom predictions laid upon my life. I am alive because I was too spiteful to accept the aborted path my mother laid out for me. Though she tried to abort me twice and suffocate me when I was nine months, I persevered. Though she strangled me and burned me, tortured me and maligned me daily I persevered. Though she beat me and broke my bones, I still loved her, believing someday I would triumph through that love. Though teachers mocked me and men defamed me, I believed through God's unfailing love I would prevail. Now, time has robbed me of my youth, and anger my gentle spirit; sorrow has taken my joy, and pain my self-respect. Pain has taken my determination, and grief my belief that I was ever destined to be successful. Fear has taken my wealth and advice has made a fool of me. "Listen to me, listen to me," they whisper in the night. "I'll show you the way," they say as they lead me down a rosy path of destruction. In contempt I ran away from those who were to teach me; abuse has controlled me while I ran. Destruction has never taken her hand off me and folly is my name. Oh, how the demons in hell must be laughing as they watched me destroy myself in a useless attempt to save me. How they rolled in hysterics as I stood "strong against them." What a fool I've been running against the wind, climbing mountains that have no top, trying to destroy dragons that were holding me their captive much like one would keep a dog on a leash. The freedom I thought I had attained I would soon find out was just the extra rope with which they allowed me to hang myself. **Though the world destroy me and folly consume me, this one thing I know: no matter what has happened or is yet to come, THE LORD GOD JEHOVAH IS ON MY SIDE!!!**

Chapter 4

Anxiety—Is it Sin?

Philippians 4:6-7 says, "Do not be anxious about anything, but in everything, by prayer and petition, with thanksgiving, present your requests to God and the peace of God, which transcends all understanding, will guard your hearts and your minds in Christ Jesus." Then we read in Matthew 11:28-9, "Come to me, all you who are weary and burdened, and I will give you rest ... you will find rest for your souls." John 16:33 suggests that " ... in Me you may have peace ... " and in John 14:1 we read, "Do not let your hearts be troubled ... Trust in God; trust also in Me." How are these scriptures to be interpreted by the Christian who struggles with the emotional response of anxiety? Is it a sign of weakened faith since such verses of scripture seem to be compelling one to avoid anxiety by putting their trust in God? Or is it a sign from the Holy Spirit to take heed for sin may have entered into one's life?

Such are the questions that haunted Elizabeth—a young person in her early twenties. Elizabeth had been referred for psychotherapy by her family physician after having attempted to treat her anxiety with appropriate medication used to reduce nervousness, anxiety, and agitation. Although briefly considering medication, Elizabeth opted for psychotherapy as an alternative since she had some fear of medications and felt that agreeing to take medication would certainly validate that her faith was weak and that she doubted God's power to heal. Elizabeth had suffered from many of the symptoms that characterize this emotional state for several years dating back to childhood. According to American Association of Christian Counselors (AACC), anxiety can be defined as a sense of dread or worry, without any concrete evidence to support these feelings. (1) Other definitions describe it as a state of being uneasy, apprehensive, or worried. When untreated, anxiety can lead to depression; recent statistics suggest that nearly 30 million persons in this country are seeking help for either anxiety or depression. Anxiety appears to be a combination of cognitive, emotional and overt actions in reaction to some perceived future event, and believing it will occur despite the lack of evidence to support its occurrence. This emotional state seems to cause the person experiencing it to ignore other possibilities, potentials, faith, and trust. The anxious person usually responds with reactivity, exaggerating the issues, and practices a rather rigid or black and white thinking. Such a person seems to miss any evidence that would help to decrease the risk of such a worry coming true.

While there are perhaps many possible causes for anxiety, Elizabeth was quite confused about the causal factors for her anxiety. She shared that she had been reared in a very good home; she reported that her parents were Christians and very loyal to their Church and the religious organizations they supported. She said she had been reared in a functional family without problems that could explain why she struggled so with anxiety on a daily basis. She reported she was unaware if either of her parents struggled with anxiety, as they never appeared to exhibit the symptoms she had tried to hide in herself. She was also unaware of anyone within the previous generations of her family who had struggled with such problems, thus not giving any evidence for a genetic predisposition or unhealthy coping skills that may have been role-modeled in her family of origin.

In taking her history, we reviewed the various physical symptoms that can accompany anxiety. These include: breathing difficulties, excessive perspiration, headaches, dizziness, tremors, palpitations of heart, restlessness, insomnia, sedation, or other disrupted sleep patterns, alterations in diet or eating, stomach-gastrointestinal difficulties, numbness, and blood pressure changes. Elizabeth agreed that she had experienced many of these physiological signs of anxiety throughout her life, but the predominant symptoms of which she struggled involved stomach-gastrointestinal difficulties, restlessness, insomnia, headaches, and at times even dizziness and tremors. She further described her symptoms to include several other emotional signs often seen with persons struggling with anxiety. These signs include: feeling tense, irritable, distraught, foreboding, a sense of anguish, apprehension, distress, dread, fear, detachment from others, impatience, panic, fear of dying, and fear of losing her mind.

Although typically with new patients experiencing such symptoms, a referral to their physician for a complete physical with blood studies is made to rule out any physiological causes that could be contributing to this problem, Elizabeth had already undergone such an evaluation. Since possible physiological factors had been ruled out as causal factors, further exploration of her life and upbringing was explored during the clinical assessment that took place at that first appointment. There are often related emotional factors that contribute toward a response of anxiety. These could include anything from feelings of inadequacy and inferiority or low self-esteem to feelings of guilt over some unresolved conflict in one's past. At times, there has been a rather traumatic event that one has repressed from their immediate thinking and recollection, but such an event can cause "trigger" memories and the anxiety that was experienced at the time of the trauma is re-experienced currently as something triggers the mind into remembering the emotions that were associated with the trauma itself. Victims of child abuse, rape or some other form of sexual victimization, observation or exposure to a tragedy or significant loss or hardship are examples of past events that might subsequently contribute to the onset of anxiety. A home environment characterized by conflict, insecurity, or frequent disruption or crisis can likewise produce the characteristic of anxiety in people as adults.

Elizabeth had already shared that she felt she had not come from a dysfunctional home. She described her parents as good Christians and her home as stable without disruption or chaos. She had not been subjected to abuse, had never been victimized sexually, nor did she feel there had been any unresolved conflict issues in her home between her parents or with her. She was an only child; she shared that she felt her parents probably "spoiled" her if anything since they certainly over-indulged her with all the conveniences they could afford. She said, "My parents desired that my life be as comfortable as possible and they made sure to provide me with things they felt I needed even if it meant they postponed purchasing something for themselves." Adding further clarification to her response, she expressed tearfully, "I have never questioned my parents love for me!"

Reassuring Elizabeth that her symptoms were quite common among Christians and many women experienced similar problems with anxiety, we concluded the initial session with prayer, asking God to give us wisdom as we explored together the possible causal factors for Elizabeth's daily struggles with anxiety. A subsequent appointment was scheduled for the next week as I told Elizabeth that we would be continuing to gather biographical information about her and her family in the next session. I had planned to do what clinicians refer to as a "genogram" in the next session. A genogram is a schematic drawing or simple outline of one's geneology and family history. This activity involves use of a large chalk board or poster to sketch out the various family members, names, ages, etc. and then enlarging the data by asking the patient to describe the various characteristics of each person on the chart. This exercise quite often is very enlightening to not only the therapist, but to the patient as well when various patterns of communication, traits, conflicts, perhaps hidden conflicts or "secrets" not openly talked about within the family system are revealed. This activity helps to obtain a picture of family dynamics; the patient can visually see possible problem areas or issues that need clarification.

Elizabeth was visibly anxious as she waited for her second session in the waiting room. Although trying to hide her anxiety, the soft nervous quiver in her voice, the sweaty palm noticed in our hand shake, and obvious discomfort gave it away as I greeted her and then requested she join me in my office. She apologized for appearing nervous, "I'm not sure why I feel so anxious coming to see you ... it isn't really anything about you or your office ... I just get this way sometimes." Reassuring her that many of the people I see experience the same thing, I directed her to a chair in front of a large poster chart and begun to draw a diagram of her family starting with her immediate family with the information from the biographical data in her chart. I then requested that we consider her grandparent's on both sides of her family; we added the individuals to complete the family tree of both her mother and father's family.

After everyone for three generations was represented on the schematic, she was asked to describe the characteristics of each person as well as provide other relevant information regarding marriages, divorces, births, deaths, vocations, and dynamics including conflicts between family members, secrets not shared with certain members of the family, and any special loyalties or bonds between certain members of the family. To dramatize the dynamics within the family structure, most therapists utilize different colors of markers such as green for loyalties or bonds between certain family members, red for conflicts, and blue and black for more generic types of information such as characteristics, age, dates of events like marriage, and death. Once finished with this activity, Elizabeth was somewhat astonished by the various colors and particularly the "green" which represented close relationships between a large number of her extended family members. There was very little "red" on the whole diagram, thus validating that Elizabeth's description of her family being fairly free of the dysfunction many families experience was accurate.

Of significance was the green circle around Elizabeth and her mother and a similar one between her mother and grandmother. Elizabeth and her mother had been quite "bonded" and as had been described by her in the initial session, she felt very protected and loved by her mother. When describing her mother, Elizabeth said she was a loving, caring person who did a lot for others. She was eager to work in the church and hardly ever declined a request from the pastor or other church leader who requested she consider assuming a needed role or position. Elizabeth said she remembers her mother saying on many of these occasions, "there is so much to be done and so few willing to do it ... I just have to accept this position (or task) since no one else will do it and if I don't, I will feel guilty!" Elizabeth shared that she felt her mother was pretty much driven by a sense of "guilt." She added that their pastor would sometimes say things like, "I'm asking you to do this since you are truly the only person we have that can fulfill this role, but think of it as doing it for God" or "let your conscience be your guide, sister … I know God will help you come to the right decision."

I suggested we digress what I had anticipated would be brief to discuss the difference between "false guilt" and "true guilt" in an effort to help Elizabeth see that the "guilt-trips" her mother's pastor used with her was probably based on false rather than true guilt. False guilt is the guilt one experiences that is man made; such guilt usually has people as its initiator or source. The source of false guilt is quite often parents, friends, or other people, and unfortunately, at times pastors. False guilt is sometimes utilized in a manipulative manner to get people to do certain things requested of them. Only true guilt comes from God; it can be convicting if one has sinned or willfully transgressed against God's Word. True guilt can also and frequently is merely an urging or prodding from the Holy Spirit that we have gone astray in our thinking or conduct; it is often a gentle nudging to get back on track. Without much further discussion, Elizabeth concluded, "What you are saying is that my mother was highly influenced by "false guilt" and that our pastor contributed toward this problem."

I agreed, but clarified, "Yes, but I'm sure your pastor meant well and didn't purposefully do this to manipulate your mother into taking on more responsibilities around the church that was feasible for her to successfully accomplish."

Elizabeth had then moved to the next observation I was about to suggest, "I guess my mother utilized some of the same tactics on me to get me to do certain things around the house or to help her in some manner." As we processed other things about the genogram, I could see that Elizabeth was becoming angrier with her mother in particular. Finally, after a short pause, she shared, "My mother did to me what her pastor did to her! She used this false guilt idea to control me or gain my cooperation in a lot of areas … that's really not right to allow someone to think their guilt is from God when it is really from another person! While I was a compliant child, I did it out of fear—fear that if I was anything but this, God would certainly be displeased and I would be stricken with more guilt. Many times, I behaved or complied with my mother's expectations from a motive of fear rather than love, respect, or a relationship … "

This simple clarification for Elizabeth produced somewhat of a catharsis for her. She began talking about specific memories she had where her mother somewhat manipulated her into compliance or participation in events or activities she would not have chosen to do if she had not feared the consequence of failing her mother who made it seem like if she failed her in any way, she was failing God Himself. I interrupted to help re-direct the session and de-escalate the anger that was building in Elizabeth toward her parents, and mother in particular. I asked her, "Do you think that your mother could have learned this technique innocently from anyone in addition to your pastor?" After some silence, I pointed to the genogram as I commented, "You might wish to look at this family map to see who influenced your mother in the family tree."

Immediately, Elizabeth responded, "My grandmother—my mother's mother!" Complimenting her for this correct observation, I once again reminded Elizabeth that this pattern that was passed down from the generations that preceded hers was quite likely not a purposeful thing—just as it had not been with her pastor.

I explained to Elizabeth that from the way she had described her mother and even the mother-daughter relationship she experienced with her, it didn't appear to me that her mother had been aggressive or selfish which would be more the precursor of a manipulative motive. In desperation to succeed in her parenting of the daughter she loved so dearly, she merely repeated things she had learned from her own upbringing. She probably wasn't able to make the connection of such practices to the guilt-driven motive that ultimately drove her to action; she probably had not been taught, nor was able to gain experience in appropriate decision making which encourages one to review all the options and ramifications prior to arriving upon a decision. Instead, she would quickly make a conclusion to avoid the discomfort that guilt feelings would produce.

Even though these emotions were produced by false guilt, they felt real and probably not much different from those produced from true guilt. These practices were then further reinforced by her pastor who in a desperate attempt to cover the various ministry needs in his small church allowed people to feel that God was calling them to a certain task if he should ask them. As explained to Elizabeth, understanding these dynamics doesn't make them less harmful or lessen the adverse effects they have had on her life, but it does allow her to forgive these people as their motive was probably correct. Understanding can also help one to stop the cycle of learning that is usually passed down from generation to generation, just as it had been from her grandmother to her mother, and then to her.

In subsequent sessions, additional observations from the genogram revealed other parenting practices or characteristics in family members that probably indirectly taught Elizabeth a response of anxiety. She was able to see that her mother and grandmother as well as a few of her aunts and uncles had experienced problems with anxiety which was somewhat masked by other things. Elizabeth concluded that she had probably been endowed with some predisposition toward anxiety since there were so many family members that experienced it to one degree or more; she also could see how through the modeling of adults in her life as a child, she learned to emulate a similar response to uncertainty, crisis, or unpredictability.

Having heard others who had gone to therapy talk about being asked to confront their parents about the conflict or injury they had caused in their life, Elizabeth reluctantly asked, "Does this mean that I should confront my mother or at least let her know I forgive her for these hang-ups she caused me?"

Elizabeth breathed a sigh of relief when I asked, "What purpose would such a confrontation have? Given the fact that your mother never did any of this intentionally, it would probably only serve to hurt her rather than change this pattern in her life." I further explained that in therapy, we sometimes encourage such confrontation of abuse, secrets, or dysfunctional patterns that continue to damage family members. However, in these cases, the confrontation is used to bring the on-going behavior to a halt and failure to do so would enable it to continue. This was not the case with Elizabeth's mother; rather than confrontation, I suggested that as her mother sees a different pattern of behavior in Elizabeth, she might start asking how she was able to accomplish feeling less anxious and thus give her the opportunity to share some of these new insights she had discovered.

Elizabeth voiced her endorsement of this plan, "I really like this idea better than confrontation since the last thing I want to do is alienate my mother from me or make her feel she failed in some way as a parent … that would only make her more anxious and it probably wouldn't help my level of anxiety either."

Learning about her family history and reviewing the parental teaching and modeling that took place in her home helped Elizabeth discover some of the sources for her anxiety. However, this only began the process necessary for learning to manage this emotional response and prevent it from interfering with her overall functioning and happiness. After several weeks of therapy and realizing that she was still struggling with anxiety more frequently than not, Elizabeth asked about the medication that her physician had suggested when contacting him initially. I explained that the source of anxiety appears to have an environmental component as well as a chemical or biological one. Recent advances in technology have produced much better information about anxiety; based on these studies, we have learned that serotonin, norepinephrine, and gamma-aminobutyric acid (GABA) networks are important chemical links to anxiety. I further explained that serotonin is one of the many natural chemicals stored in the nerves and essentially facilitates sending messages (electrical impulses) to other cells throughout the body. Since serotonin helps to carry the message from one nerve cell to another, it is also called a neurotransmitter. While serotonin regulates our emotional reactions to relationships and the environment, norepinephrine is an adrenaline type substance that seems connected to energy level and alertness. GABA is the brain's natural chemical substance that calms or has a tranquilizing effect. Dysfunction in any of these systems can result in anxiety, irrational fears, panic, or bizarre physiological reactions.

As explained to Elizabeth, we are so fortunate to now have available to us medications that can help to re-stabilize these systems when they have been disrupted. Medications such as

Prozac (fluoxetine), Zoloft (sertraline), Paxil (paroxetine), Celexa (citalopram), Luvox (fluvoxamine), and the most recently developed Lexapro (escitalopram) are serotonin facilitating antidepressants (SSRI's) which are usually the first line of attack for anxiety and depressive symptoms. These medications are not addictive in nature and are usually easily managed by one's physician. Typically, the drug is started at a very low dosage and slowly increased upward to the target dosage; symptom reduction is often seen within two to three weeks. Although some people experience side effects (nausea, diarrhea, insomnia, fatigue, or reduced sexual libido), we have learned that side effects are usually related to dosing. By starting at lower doses and increasing gradually, most people do not experience side effects. Other medications include tricyclic antidepressants such as Tofranil (imipramine), but its usefulness is limited due to several side effects such as weight gain, dry mouth, drowsiness, and lowered blood pressure. It, as well as other tricyclic antidepressants, can be toxic in overdose situations. While not utilized very much any more since the newer developed medications are easier to manage with few side effects, MAO inhibitors such as Nardil (phenelzine), Parnate (tranylcypromine) and Marplan (isocarbozazid), were previously used to treat anxiety and panic attacks. This class of medications is not popular since they require adherence to a very strict diet to prevent potentially fatal reactions as they interact severely with other medications and even some foods. Effexor (venlafaxine) is an antidepressant medication that is approved for treating anxiety; it regulates serotonin and norepinephrine in the brain. Another class of medications known as Benzodiazepine medications such as Xanax (alprazolam), Ativan (lorazepam), and Klonopin (clonazepam) are useful in treating anxiety; while effective immediately, they must be kept to short-term usage since they can be addictive and can cause significant sedation and cognitive impairment. Low dose beta-blocker medications such as Inderal (propranolol) are also sometimes used to reduce anxiety symptoms especially in social anxiety and stage fright situations.

After this explanation, Elizabeth remembered that her physician had initially suggested she consider the medication called Effexor.

She said, "My doctor wanted me to try Effexor, but I was uncomfortable with this as I had heard that such medications do strange things with your mind and that they are addictive. I also remember that my mother would never take medications even though her doctor suggested it ... she said that her faith in God was strong enough to handle her problems and to take medication would mean her faith was too weak."

Careful to reassure Elizabeth's bold step in even considering the option of medication, which defied earlier learning, I said, "This is one of the many myths some Christian people have about medication. I usually try to explain that needing to take a safe medication for anxiety or depression is no different, nor shows any less faith than to take insulin when one is diabetic." I then further explained that a chemical imbalance or decreased level of a needed hormone or chemical in the body is not much different than the diabetic who experiences a body that does not produce the needed insulin that he or she needs to function properly. "God would not expect the diabetic to increase his or her faith ... He would desire that they be willing to take the substance that their body requires (insulin) and show wisdom by doing so!" I added. "Furthermore, I really think that God expects us to take advantage of the various things He has helped mankind develop to facilitate healing ... while God is certainly capable of healing us instantaneously without any medical intervention, I feel that He typically brings healing to us through traditional methods of medicine, including surgery, therapy, medications, and related treatment approaches." At the conclusion of this discussion, Elizabeth indicated she was now ready to start the Effexor while continuing psychotherapy. A phone call was made to her physician and arrangements were made for her prescription of this medication.

It was probably the combination of appropriate medication and psychotherapy that helped Elizabeth significantly reduce the anxiety in her life. She was also encouraged to begin reading good Christian literature on the topic of anxiety. The first book she chose to read was perhaps one that is frequently referenced by Christian therapists—Happiness Is A Choice, co-authored by Drs. Frank Minirth and Paul Meier, both Christian psychiatrists who founded the Minirth-Meier Clinic. Many of the following helpful coping skills we discussed in subsequent sessions are suggested in this excellent resource: (2)

- **Learn to live one day at a time:** Matthew 6:34 suggests that we don't have to worry about tomorrow since God will take care of us and all our tomorrows. Experts in the field of anxiety report that 80% of the things people tend to worry about will never come true. Practice the art of learning to live one day at a time.
- **Set time limits on your worries:** By scheduling a time to think about problems or worries each day, we can begin to put limits on the time wasted in worrying. This will allow more focused time for other activities that can be more productive and relaxing—thus stress reducing.
- **Avoid procrastination:** Putting things off and then having insufficient time to complete the task or trying to beat a deadline only increases anxiety and worry ... PLAN AHEAD!
- **Get adequate recreation:** Most people need at least 3 to 4 times of recreation per week to help reduce their level of stress.
- **Get adequate rest and sleep:** Avoid becoming overly tired or sleepy as it reduces efficiency and can increase anxiety and stress.
- **Get adequate exercise:** Ideally, we should plan to exercise at least 3 to 4 times per week. Exercise helps improve overall physical health as well as reduces stress; it is a good diversion for worrying or anxiety.
- **Talk to a close friend at least once per week about your frustrations:** Everyone can benefit from a support person who will listen to his or her frustrations; a prayer partner can be a good support person for listening as well as helping you pray about concerns that could escalate into worries.
- **Listen to good wholesome Christian Music:** Music is

an excellent modality for reducing stress and anxiety in one's life. Soft, tranquil, peaceful music can be a diversion to worrying and fretting about problems; music can provide needed respite for the troubled soul.

- **Confront fears or worries directly:** After identifying the fear or worry, examine different alternatives or options for resolution. Finally, make efforts to reach solutions by trying the various options until finding one that helps to bring relief.
- **Focus on scriptural meditations that help to reduce anxiety:** There are several references in scripture that can be helpful in reducing specific fears or worries. Some of these examples follow:
  - (Phil. 4:7 "peace of God, which transcends all understanding, will guard your hearts and your mind ... ") **Realize that God can keep our mind safe as we obey Him!**
  - (Phil 4:8 " ... whatever is true ... noble ... right ... pure ... lovely ... admirable ... excellent or praiseworthy ... think about such things") **Meditate on positive thoughts!**
  - **Focus on Godly behavior** (Phil. 4:9) **by avoiding sin** (Prov. 4:15) **and joining small fellowship groups** (Heb. 10:24-5)
  - (Phil. 4:8 " ... whatever is noble ... right ... pure ... lovely ... think about such things ... ") **Divert attention from self to others!**
  - (Phil. 4:6 " ... do not be anxious about anything, but in everything by prayer and petition ... present your requests to God") **Determine to obey God! Pray! Adopt a philosophy of "Why worry when you can pray?"**
  - (Phil. 4:11 " ... for I have learned to be content whatever the circumstances" and I Tim. 6:6 " ... godliness with contentment is great gain") **Work on being content! Practice the art of positive thinking! Redefine problems as challenges or**

opportunities to grow! Turn the lemons life deals you into lemonade!

- (Phil. 4:13 "I can do everything through him who gives me strength") **Realize there is a twofold responsibility—yours and Christ's—in doing everything!**
- (Phil. 4:19 "And my God will meet all your needs according to his glorious riches in Christ Jesus") **Eliminate the worry of poverty; God promises to supply all our needs!**
- (Phil. 4:23 "the grace of the Lord Jesus Christ be with your spirit") **Realize that the grace of God is with you! Accept the sufficiency of God's grace for whatever you face!**

Over the course of six months, starting with weekly sessions and then progressing to every other week, Elizabeth completed treatment for her anxiety disorder. After beginning the appropriate medication, her symptoms became more manageable which permitted her to be more focused on changing her beliefs about the anxiety that seemed to have robbed her of the peace and happiness that God desired she have in Him. Through expanded knowledge of this problem, the causal and contributing factors, and the development of coping skills for managing the normal anxiety that everyone experiences, Elizabeth conquered it. Without becoming resentful toward her mother, who had innocently passed on false teaching or beliefs about anxiety that she had accepted as absolute truth, Elizabeth altered her beliefs about anxiety. She was even able to come to the conclusion that anxiety is a natural emotional state and that some anxiety is realistic and healthy as reflected in Philippians 2:20 as "a genuine interest" or in I Corinthians 12:25 and II Corinthians 11:28 as "concern."

This normal state of anxiety can be one's friend and does not have to be avoided or considered bad. Elizabeth learned that it is anxiety that helped her avoid certain things that could endanger her life and was instrumental in helping to keep her safe and make wise decisions regarding her welfare. However, as Elizabeth's story documents, if this normal emotional state gets out of balance and becomes excessive, it can become harmful. The excessive anxiety, reflected in Luke 8:14 as " ... choked by life's worries ... " seems to describe the person like Elizabeth who is overwhelmed with anxiety and not seemingly capable of enjoying the peace that God desires for His children. Although previously feeling that she was failing God by experiencing excessive anxiety, she learned this was not true; Elizabeth came to an understanding that such feelings were misinterpretations or faulty conclusions she had drawn. She also began to interpret verses like Philippians 4:6 that exhort "Do not be anxious about anything ... " or I Peter 5:7 that says to " ... cast all your anxiety on him ... " differently. Prior to addressing her problems with anxiety, she interpreted these verses literally; since she seemed to be failing at casting her anxiety on God or being anxious in nothing, she concluded she was sinning and certainly seen as a failure to God. She struggled with the concept of faith, feeling that if her faith had been stronger, perhaps then she would be able to cast her cares and anxieties onto God. Now, she could see that anxiety is more often a medical problem with legitimate causes that can be treated. She began seeing that these scriptures, rather than to condemn her, had the goal of giving her hope. As a Christian, God desired to help her with her anxiety; these scripture references started bringing comfort to her troubled soul rather than condemnation.

What a wonderful ending to her story—through the combined approaches of medication and psychotherapy, Elizabeth conquered what had kept her captive for so many years; and, now she no longer is threatened by anxiety. After eight months, she was able to discontinue the medication as her body's chemical balance had re-stabilized and she no longer needed the medication. However, she shares with others that if she should relapse or feel she could bene-fit from medication again, she would not hesitate to resume taking it. In speaking about anxiety, she now describes it as a normal part of life for many people; she has accepted that she may always have some tendencies toward this emotional response at times of stress or some other disruption of normal routines in her life, but she no longer becomes overwhelmed or incapacitated by it. Elizabeth says,

"With God's help, I have broadened my understanding of this emotion; I've changed the misperceptions and conclusions that I had drawn from previous learning and experiences. I no longer see anxiety as 'sin' or a 'lack of faith' or even something God is using to teach me or draw me closer to Him. Through some traditional means involving both medication and therapy, God has brought healing to my life ... I have victory over anxiety!"

Chapter 5

Proper Self Esteem vs. Selfish Pride

Referred to as an epidemic within the church by Dr. James Dobson in several of his writings, proper self-esteem vs. selfish pride needs to be discussed. Perhaps the church in general and both well meaning pastors and laypersons have not sufficiently addressed the importance of good self-esteem for one's overall healthy emotional adjustment. Far too often, it is either emphasized as more important than the message of holiness which is also referred to as "perfect love" or confused with "selfish pride" which the Bible describes as sin. Although an error in their thinking multitudes of Christian people who are truly seeking God's perfect will for their lives, have concluded that any kind of self-acceptance or appreciation for the God-given attributes they possess is wrong and not pleasing to God.

While clinicians may see a higher proportion of women who experience low self-esteem, there could very likely be similar numbers of men who likewise struggle with this issue. Women are more willing to share their inner most feelings with others; men generally keep these thoughts and feelings to themselves, feeling that any expression of such doubts would certainly convey a negative view of their manhood. Accepting one's own attributes and utilizing them for advancing the Kingdom is very different than selfish pride which the Bible describes as carnal.

Differences between selfish pride and self-esteem is probably more confusing to the unsanctified person; however, for those who are totally surrendered to God through that second work of grace known as sanctification, acceptance of the God-given talents and giving Him all the glory for such attributes can be more easily understood and accomplished. A person with selfish pride has an attitude of getting ahead no matter whom they have to step on to reach their goal. This type of pride is sin; the Bible clearly warns against such an attitude throughout scriptures. Proverbs 11:2 warns, " ... when pride comes, then comes disgrace; in Proverbs 16:18, we read, "pride goes before destruction, a haughty spirit before a fall; and finally in Proverbs 29:23, we see that "a man's pride brings him low ... ." Pride is further understood as conveyed by Paul in Philippians 2:3 when he admonishes, "do nothing out of selfish ambition or vain conceit, but in humility consider others better than yourselves." Thinking of others by humbling ourselves and taking on the attitude of a servant that we might win them to Christ or minister to their needs does not imply we must avoid self-acceptance or an appreciation for the talents God has endowed us with to accomplish this goal. Selfish pride is further described in James 3:14 as "selfish ambition" and we are warned in 3:16 that this feeling "does not come down from heaven, but is earthly, unspiritual, and of the devil."

Achieving and maintaining good self-esteem is accepting God's blessing to us and enables us to be fit for accomplishing His call upon our life. Galations 6:4 admonishes one to "test his own actions ... then he can take pride in himself without comparing himself to somebody else." What Paul is describing here is an acceptance of oneself or self-esteem; he is saying it's okay to have this kind of pride for it is not selfish or self-centered—it is merely allowing one to become more self-confident in what God has allowed him or her to accomplish for the Kingdom. This form of pride is not competitive in nature, for it suggests that self evaluation and improvement rather than comparison to others is good. In James 1:9, we read that a "brother in humble circumstances ought to take pride in his high position ... ." The key to a balanced view of pride seems to involve remaining humble and totally committed to God; for in sanctification, the believer recognizes that it is only through God that he or she accomplishes anything. Song writers have tried to convey this thought in their creations throughout history in such songs as "Oh, For A Thousand Tongues To Sing" and "To God Be The Glory ... Great Things He Hath Done" and "Without Him I Could Do Nothing."

The second commandment, given to Moses, commands us as Christians to "Love your neighbor as yourself" (Luke 10:27) and this command clearly sets as a pre-requisite that "loving oneself" to some degree is necessary before one can really know how to love his or her neighbor. To deny oneself of self-acceptance is to minimize the creation and God's desire and plan to bless mankind. Genesis 1:27 documents that "God created man in his own image ... in the image of God he created him." Further down in that same chapter that documents the creation, we read, "God blessed them ... and God saw all that he had made, and it was very good." God created man in his own image, unlike all other parts of His creation. Persons who deny themselves positive self-esteem are essentially questioning God's Word. His Word clearly proclaims that God's creation which involved man and the attributes endowed him by the Creator were good.

Perhaps much of the confusion surrounding the concept of self-esteem, self-worth, or self-image, is the result of using these terms synonymously with "self-love". These are not equal terms; and, they are far more different than similar! Webster (96) defines self-esteem as "self-respect" and self-worth as "the sense of one's own value or worth as a person; self-esteem, self-respect, or self-worthiness." (1) Adding further clarity to the meaning of these words is the definition of self-image which Webster defines as "the conception or mental image one has of oneself." (2) All of these definitions suggest the importance of self-regard which is a "consideration of oneself or one's interests and self-respect" (Webster, 96). (3) On the contrary, Webster defines self-love as "the instinct or tendency to promote one's own welfare or well-being ... an excessive regard for one's own advantage and interests ... conceit, vanity." (4) Self-love is not the acceptance of one's own attributes, but an excessive regard for one's interests and tendency to promote one's own well-being or interests—a selfish or self-centeredness that scripture warns against. While self-esteem is a balanced view of oneself and involves an appreciation for the gifts and attributes God has allowed him or her to enjoy, self-love is an exaggerated view of oneself—perhaps a carnal desire to succeed above others and a willingness to compromise values to achieve those selfish interests.

Having grown up in a minister's home and hearing hundreds of sermons on how to be a good Christian, Susan had struggled with uncertainty and feelings of inadequacy her entire life. During her teenage years, she had hoped that once reaching adulthood, she would struggle less with these feelings that seemed to stifle her ability to feel successful in anything she tried to accomplish. She had read most of the self-help books available concerning self image and self-esteem; however like literally thousands of others in the church, she remained confused over this issue. Susan was a genuine Christian; she had an active devotional life that was a consistent part of her daily schedule. She attended church regularly and special services, retreats, camps, and such events whenever she had such opportunities. Her pursuit of God's will for her life was genuine; her commitment to God and living a life of holiness was unquestionable by anyone who knew her.

Finally, after surviving the challenges of teenage years, completing college, and marrying the man of her dreams and starting a family, she decided that she would seek professional help in desperation to find some answers to what she described as "low self-esteem." Susan shared quite openly on that first appointment that she had hoped that her feelings of inadequacy would diminish after teenage years, but she only found more frustration as she entered college and found herself now competing for dates with the few available single guys who also attended the small Bible College where she had enrolled. "It wasn't that I struggled academically or even socially ... I made good grades and found the studies not too difficult ... I dated as much as other girls in my dorm and didn't seem to have trouble getting asked out for dates," she shared as tears began to form under both eyelids. Attempting to hold back the tears as she apologized for crying, she began to describe the confusion she felt within, "God really blessed me with a great Christian family, I was reared in a parsonage and have a wonderful family and Christian heritage on both sides for several generations back ... I was blessed with much more than many of my peers ... I fell in love with a wonderful Christian guy who is the best husband and father that any woman could have ... we have two beautiful children who are healthy, we have good jobs, we don't suffer from any physical or health problems ... why can't I feel happy about these things without feeling guilty?"

Susan was an attractive woman in her mid thirties with a professional and quite pleasant appearance; although she had given birth to two children, she had not allowed herself to become overweight. It was obvious that she practiced good hygiene and good self-discipline with regard to diet and nutrition. She quite likely made her husband look good when they were together as a couple. Although she seemed to have a radiance of personality about her demeanor, an inner turmoil and sadness could be detected upon closer examination. Like many Christians struggling with low self-esteem, Susan had developed some coping skills or a facade that adequately hid the feelings of inadequacy, insecurity, and worthlessness that had become a daily part of her life. Susan was extremely fearful of becoming "prideful" as she described what her parents had fiercely warned her and her siblings about. She shared, "my mother dressed very modestly and insisted that we girls also dress with rather drab colors and sometimes outdated styles to avoid being seen by others as "flashy or gaudy." Susan admitted that she struggled with feeling self-conscience about the clothing she wore to school as it seemed so plain in comparison to the other students' attire. After sharing these thoughts, Susan quickly explained that she didn't mean to be criticizing her parents and she didn't wish for me to get the wrong impression of them. She added, "They really raised us the best they knew how ... they really felt what they were doing was right ... I don't hold them responsible for my problems now." Susan then explained that while she didn't blame her parents for her issues, she had decided to change some practices in raising her own two children. Although still insisting that her two daughters dress modestly, she said that she takes pride in helping them select fashionable and attractive outfits for school. She expressed how still maintaining modesty, she wanted their children to feel they could fit in with peers and not stand out as "weird" or "odd."

We discussed several things that may have contributed to Susan's thinking, thus leading her to formulate these false conclusions about herself. As pointed out to her, Satan very seldom tempts a committed Christian like herself with outright sin—for such a person would never knowingly commit such a transgression against God. However, if he can cause one to doubt his or her experience with Christ—to question their spirituality, so to speak—then he can bring discouragement and feelings of inadequacy and defeat, which ultimately stifles their sense of peace and contentment. Finally, this process can lead to depression; the person feels powerless to change or ever meet up to the expectations they feel they must meet in order to feel acceptable. They have fallen into what some clinicians term "the performance trap" or the feeling that their performance is inferior and will probably never measure up to what would be considered acceptable by God or others. Such individuals will often tell their therapists, "I'm not smart enough ... talented enough ... tall enough ... thin enough ... strong enough" among other rationalizations they have come to believe as causal factors for this sense of failure.

As we continued our discussion, I suggested to Susan that if Satan could get her to believe a lie that she was inadequate and would never measure up to God's standards, then she would eventually lose her sense of motivation and become pessimistic. Since people are subject to human feelings and emotional reactions, Satan quite likely recognizes that most of us make choices and act based not on logic or our thinking, but rather on the basis of our emotions or how we feel. Advertisers have utilized this observation for years in the advertising field; they make us think that we absolutely need something and expose our appetites in a manner that urges us to choose their product on an emotional basis rather than thinking through the options logically. If Satan is successful in causing us to accept this lie, then our subsequent behavior is one of defeat and discouragement. Some eventually give up trying and reject God.

Fortunately, Susan had not given up; but she had continued to struggle daily against the emotional feelings that caused her to feel unsuccessful in many aspects of her Christian experience and life. As suggested to Susan, if we can think logically, with our conclusions based on the ultimate truth—God's Word—then we can overcome the emotions we are experiencing at the time and proceed with decision making that is more logical and less emotional in nature. Emotions can be confusing and the result of any number of things such as exhaustion, physical illnesses, side effects to prescribed medications, reactions to trauma or a crisis in life, and a chemical imbalance within our body as well as other contributing causal factors. This is the reason our decision making should be based on logical thinking rather than the way we feel or emotions.

Susan agreed that she most likely had fallen into that trap several years before as she frequently felt doomed to accept her achievement as inadequate in comparison to peers who seemed to feel more fulfilled than she did. As we discussed this concept of performance and God's expectations on us as His children, I reminded Susan that God judges our motive—not our performance. I further illustrated this to mean that if God was calling me into the ministry, and it took me 6 months to refine that call on my life through prayer and meditation in His word and through consultation with my pastor and church leaders, God would be just as pleased with me as He was with another man that had come to the same conclusion and responded to God's call on his life within 3 months. The issue is not the time it takes to firm up our decision—or performance—but the motive of one's heart. If I am truly committed to God and seeking His will in my life, remaining open to His direction and diligently seeking answers, then God considers my heart pure. If my heart and motive is correct—then my performance is satisfactory to God! I reminded Susan that ultimately, we are serving God—not mankind. Quite often, our peers will set standards for successful performance and if we are not careful, we fall into the trap of trying to meet up to those standards, rather than focusing on keeping our heart open to God's direction and control in our lives.

Attempting to validate her on that first appointment, I shared that her issues were very common among women in the church and how Dr. James Dobson had referenced this problem as an epidemic within the church. Being reminded that others experienced similar feelings and Dr. Dobson addressing this issue as a leader within the religious community, seemed to give further credibility to her confusion. I could detect some optimism and hope as I shared with her that I had seen countless numbers of women and some men with similar problems. I further suggested that with God's help, I was confident that she could overcome these feelings and find acceptance and a level of contentment with herself. As the session was coming to an end, I asked Susan to begin working on a definition of self-esteem and suggested that she might also look at words that would be considered synonyms such as "self-worth," "self-image," and "self-regard." I explained that in her next session we would begin a comparison of definitions of these words with the definition of "self-love." I encouraged her to look at both secular references such as a basic Webster's Dictionary definition as well as verses of scripture that contained these words as referenced in her Bible's concordance. We closed the session with prayer, asking God to begin the process of expanding Susan's understanding of herself and that He would give direction to our efforts at helping her attain a more positive self-perception.

Although still troubled by low self-esteem and confused by her feelings, Susan left that first session with more hope that she would resolve the confusion in her mind. She was anxious to schedule her second session soon and assured me that she could have her homework done within just a few days. Her excitement for further sessions seemed to indicate an investment and motivation in therapy—both good signs that lead to a favorable prognosis for reaching therapy goals. She was encouraged to share our discussion with her husband and invite him to join her in the next session if possible; his support and encouragement would be vitally important during the process of treatment. He rearranged his work schedule and they arranged for the girls to spend some time with their grandparents which made it possible for him to join his wife in her next session. He was most complimentary of Susan as we began small talk in the beginning of the session. It was obvious to me that this young man had a deep and unconditional love for his wife; he expressed his hope that Susan could feel more positive about herself and recognize the multitude of things she does for her family and others.

As we reviewed the definitions and scriptural references related to this issue as discussed above, Susan and her husband began gaining insights that broadened their understanding of the importance of having positive self-esteem and how it contributes to good emotional adjustment. When I was sure that both Susan and her husband understood the difference between "self- esteem" and "self love," I explained to them that part of the confusion surrounding this concept is the result of the psychology field itself. Becoming a major force in society in the early 1970's, psychology seemed to become a "buzz" word in every household. It was during this time that many of what had previously been thought as causal factors for emotional problems were overly simplified; this new wave of philosophical thought indicated that a majority of problems exhibited by people in our society was the result of having low self-esteem or not having sufficient love for oneself.

Leaders in the psychology field given credit for developing this theory included Eric Fromm who was a professed secular humanist and later Carl Rogers who popularized Fromm's theory and "fathered" the great self-help movement in society today. Among the many problems with accepting a secular psychological perspective is the exclusion of the scriptural concept of original sin or the adamic nature which suggests that man basically is bad until he allows God to become a part of his life. Secular psychology would disagree, stating that man is basically good and that if man is taught to love himself sufficiently, he will not cause problems in society. In fact, Fromm's theory suggests that if man sufficiently loves himself, he has his own internal guidance system that helps him make right decisions! I further shared that in my opinion, many pastors and church leaders vehemently disagreed with this secular movement—and rightly so as it was contrary to scripture. However, those who disagreed may have gone too far in their attempt to avoid contamination from this secular movement and any reference to self acceptance, self-image, self-esteem or self-regard were equated with "self-love" rather than searching for a more balanced view. Perhaps the over-reaction of these men and women was further promoted by the compromise in truth that they saw occurring in many churches and from many pulpits. In a sermon entitled "Self-Love" (1997) at Mount of Praise Camp Meeting, Dr. Thomas Hermiz claimed that most people attending our churches are familiar with the importance of self-esteem but are not familiar with the terminology of holiness, sanctification, or the concept of heart holiness that can provide one with "perfect love."(5) Dr. Hermiz claims that instead of preaching on "perfect love", a multitude of pastors began preaching on the importance of self-esteem which essentially compromised our doctrine of heart holiness. Perhaps it was more fashionable to preach on the importance of self-worth rather than the manner in which one can achieve a healthy view of oneself through the second work of grace known as sanctification or "perfect love."

Over the next several months, weekly sessions were scheduled with Susan and her husband. As their understanding about self esteem deepened, Susan's acceptance of the importance of self-esteem in her life became much easier. She grew to appreciate a concept most therapists use in their work with people—the concept that "knowledge is powerful." With expanded knowledge of a subject, one can begin to let go of previously held notions and even myths about the subject that over the years become conditioned in their mind as being absolute truth. Without faulting Susan's parental teaching against any form of self-acceptance, she was challenged to begin developing her own view of this subject matter. Through therapy sessions and her own pursuit of deepening her knowledge of this topic, Susan began forming her own viewpoint and philosophy that she could apply to her life.

With a more balanced view of self-esteem, Susan's previous guilt feelings that had become associated with any feeling of self-confidence and stifled a more positive sense of self-worth became less frequent. She soon gained the ability to quickly evaluate the appropriateness of the sense of guilt that might follow some accomplishment or successful performance on her part. She was challenged to use the following questions as an evaluative format for such times:

1. Am I doing this out of jealousy or a competitive attitude that I wish to be better than others?
2. Have I compromised values or integrity in any way to accomplish this goal?
3. Am I taking personal credit for this accomplishment and wish to be recognized for such accomplishment or performance without recognizing that such talents, attributes, or abilities only come from God?
4. Is my motive one of selfish ambition rather than out of a heart of love and service to others?

As explained to Susan, if the answer to any of the above four questions was "yes", then she needed to further assess the situation and her attitude; an affirmative answer to these questions might indicate an attitude of "self-love" which she wanted to avoid. However, if she could answer "no" to the questions, she could assume that the feelings of guilt she might be having were quite likely "false guilt" and not from the Holy Spirit but a result of the previous false learning that caused her to feel that any positive regard of herself certainly reflected a carnal "self-love." She was challenged to then express her thanks to God for the opportunity of serving in the Kingdom through sharing the talents, attributes, and abilities He had provided her. Within time, Susan began to replace the myths that had served to distort her view of "self-esteem" and she clearly learned the differences between "self-esteem" and "self-love." Although she would occasionally tend to relapse and have times of self-doubt, the frequency of these times lessened over time and the duration of such episodes were much shorter than the days and weeks that previously characterized such times of turmoil.

Upon gaining confidence in her new understanding of self-esteem and its importance in the overall balance for emotional stability, Susan then asked if we could change the focus of a few sessions to involve how to teach her children the correct application of self-esteem in their lives. She further explained, "I don't wish to repeat some of the false learning that I have been exposed to ... I certainly don't wish for them to go through what I have gone through ... but at the same time, I don't want to leave their under-standing of it to the secular psychology movement that probably characterizes anything they will get at the public school." Susan wisely conveyed that she wanted to take responsibility for teaching her children about the importance of self-esteem. I agreed that this would be a good direction for our therapy sessions as it would only further validate the gains Susan had made in therapy.

She seemed somewhat surprised when I asked, "Why would you want to improve on what you already do so well?" After a brief silence, I decided to continue my explanation by elaborating, "Your husband has described you as a very complimentary mother and wife; while you tend to see the good in everybody else, it was hard for you to see it in yourself! You have significantly contributed in developing good self-esteem in your girls through your daily affirmation of them—they know you love them and are very proud of their accomplishments and willingness to put God first place in their lives. Your husband has shared in multiple sessions how he feels so appreciated by you; he said that you tend to focus on his accomplishments, express your appreciation for his leadership, and look over the things he feels he does less adequately."

Still somewhat confused by this feedback, I reminded Susan that it is often very hard for people suffering from low self-esteem to accept complimentary comments from others. They tend to reject the compliment entirely, minimize it, or conclude that the other person is merely trying to make them feel better; they often come to a false conclusion that while they are being complimentary, they don't really feel that way. I reminded Susan that another change she should seriously consider would be to begin believing people when they gave her positive feedback. At this point, I got an idea that I felt might help to prove this point with Susan as well as further vali-date her importance as a wife and mother. I asked her if she would accept my challenge of conducting an experiment over this next week with her children and husband. She cautiously asked, "What would this experiment entail?"

Complimenting her for her caution prior to agreeing to comply, I responded to her question, "Oh, it will be easy … much easier than any of the other homework you have completed." I further explained that I wanted her to ask each of her two girls to write down the ten best things they liked about her as their mother. Additionally, she was requested to do the same with her husband with a slight alteration of the assignment—he was to write down the ten best things he valued in her as a mother and the ten best things he valued in her as a wife. As you might suspect, Susan—a very sincere and motivated patient—agreed to do this experiment.

The next session took place about a week later; I was probably about as excited as I thought Susan would be as I could predict with a high degree of accuracy what would take place in that session. True to my expectations, Susan presented that day with a genuine smile on her face that markedly differed from one her facade provided in the earlier sessions. She expressed, "I'm really embarrassed to give you these lists; I think my kids and husband really outdid themselves … I can't be as good as they have described me!"

Susan's husband interrupted by directing a comment to his wife, "Honey, I've been trying to tell you for years, you are the best thing than has ever happened to me; you are the best mother that I could ever hope and pray that my children would have!"

Complimenting her husband's affirmation of her, I then added, "Susan, if this is what they have expressed in writing—how much more do they feel that they just couldn't express in written words?" I then added, " … and I think your therapist suggested you are supposed to begin believing people when they give you positive feedback." I further explained that all of us have multiple opportunities daily to influence others through our expressions of kindness, love, and concern. We probably influence thousands of people in significantly positive ways throughout our lives that we will never know about. We can only assume and hope that our influences were of a positive nature—one that reflects Christ!

As we further discussed Susan's concern that she develop a plan of action for insuring that as parents they would help their two daughters develop a healthy self-esteem and balanced view of themselves with an acceptance of the many talents and attributes

God had given them, we decided to make a list of things they could do that would help them meet this goal. The list follows:

1. Be complimentary—try to use twice as many compliments for acceptable behavior or successful performance as confrontation of misbehavior or challenges to improve performance. All of us need compliments; most of us know that we are much more apt to try harder from praise than from negative feedback. Genuine, heartfelt praise for worthy accomplishments has no substitutes for it encourages a willingness to try new activities and more difficult goals.

2. Ask you child's opinion when appropriate—this allows the child to have a sense of importance and that his or her feelings are important to parents, family, and peers. Be cautious not to criticize the child's opinions—they are as valid as any of our opinions; if the opinion is based on wrong conclusions, then it is an opportunity for the parent to clarify things without discounting the child's thoughts.

3. Pray with and for your child—this helps your child realize he or she is important to you and to God. The opportunity to model the importance of a consistent prayer life and seeking God's direction in all of life's decisions is perhaps one of the greatest lessons a parent can teach their son or daughter. Thanking God for your children allows them to feel they have been a gift or blessing to you from God.

4. Answer your child's questions—children learn by asking questions and they have the right to have their questions answered. By encouraging the child to ask questions, a parent is conveying that questions are okay and by seeking answers to our questions, we can grow and mature. Parents should try to answer a child's questions as honestly as they can—sometimes saying, "I don't know." Parents don't have to know all the answers; to admit they don't know helps to model humility.

Parents should answer their child's questions with detail appropriate to the developmental level of the child and in a manner that would benefit the child. When questions are handled appropriately by parents, children then get the message that asking questions is okay.

5. Keep your promises—a kept promise is an example of truth to a child. A kept promise is a great act of love for it conveys to the child that he or she is loved and valued by the parent enough that when a promise is made, it is kept. Kept promises help the child develop a sense of trust and security in his parent's word; promises not kept teach distrust and produce insecurity.

6. Give reasons for your decisions—whenever possible, give a reason or explanation for a request or rule that is set by the parent. While avoiding basing the reason on absolutes ("because I'm the parent and you're the kid ... "), it's okay to explain the reason to be "because we love you so much we want to protect you ... keep you safe ... etc." A child who is given explanations comes to feel he or she is worthy of consideration when decisions are made in the family.

7. Allow the child to teach sometimes—give your child opportunities to teach you something he or she knows. Nothing gives the child a greater "high" than to know something well enough to teach someone else—especially an adult. By taking time to listen to your child's story, explanation, or new learning, a parent conveys they are of value and importance.

8. Be willing to apologize to your child—parents should never hesitate to apologize to their children when they have disappointed, hurt, or failed them in some way. By asking forgiveness, the parent is modeling humility and that parents are not perfect. Not only does apologizing to the child model the importance of admitting wrong and taking responsibility for it, but it also expresses the importance of that child's relationship with the parent.

9. Say, "I love you"—parents should never assume that their child knows they are loved. Love is the foundation on which self-esteem is built. Frequent and continuous affirmation of a parent's love for their child is important. When children question the love for them, they will also have difficulty feeling they have value.

As we finished our list of possible ways to enhance their children's self-esteem as parents, we realized that the time for that session was coming to a close. Susan rapidly copied these items down for further reference; I suggested that if she and her husband thought of other things over this next week, they could add to this list and we would discuss those items further in the next session. As we concluded that session, I suggested to Susan and her husband, "Perhaps one of the best ways to teach self-esteem to our children is to model it ourselves. As you think of this list and other possible additions over this coming week, why don't you also think of ways you can model this concept in your own life so that your daughters can see it in your example?" They agreed.

The next session took place a couple of weeks later as the sessions had began occurring on a less frequent basis due to Susan's progress. At that session we added the following items as suggestions that would help them as adults model a positive level of self-esteem:

1. **Take a personal inventory**—list one's assets (talents, abilities, skills, etc.) as well as liabilities (weaknesses) and compare the list. Usually, one will find the list of assets will far outweigh the liabilities.
2. **Acknowledge your strengths**—rather than reinforce feelings of inadequacy by making "put-down" statements about yourself or abilities, begin recognizing your strengths and focus on these rather than weaknesses. Begin to believe what others tell you about your attributes, rather than assuming they are just trying to make you feel good.
3. **Make a plan or strategy**—set some realistic goals

and begin working toward them. Determine how you can make use of your assets or strengths to assist with improvement of weaker performance areas. By establishing a fairly consistent routine, self-discipline and task completion become easier; a sense of fulfillment and satisfaction comes from completing planned tasks.

4. **Stop Comparing performance to others**—rather than compare your performance to others, learn to compare your performance with your own performance over time. Progress should be measured by taking a baseline, setting goals for improvement, then re-measuring performance and comparing it to the baseline data. There will always be others who can perform better than you in a particular area; however, you will likely show strengths in other areas where they do not. Learn to accept your assets as your unique abilities that have been provided by God.

5. **Adopt healthy habits**—people who experience high self-esteem usually are self-disciplined in taking care of themselves while those with low self-esteem neglect caring for themselves. Maintain a balance in eating, sleeping, work, and exercise. Taking time to relax helps to re-fuel and prepares one to better handle future challenges. There is probably some truth to the cliché "early to bed, early to rise, makes a man healthy, wealthy, and wise ... "

6. **Start giving to others**—people discover that by helping others, they can enhance their own sense of self-worth. Perhaps by beginning to focus on others, one realizes that others may be worse off than they are themselves; they also recognize that their help makes a difference.

7. **Begin forming a positive outlook on life**—looking for the positives in any given situation will help the negative look less bleak. By accepting the philosophy that "problems are opportunities" a more optimistic outlook

is possible. Develop a whole new philosophy for life;
rather than looking at a problem or uncomfortable challenge as having been dealt a lemon, take that lemon and
make lemonade.

Susan commented, "I really need to work on some of these,
especially the one about avoiding comparing performance to others;
I guess if I were to evaluate my progress in what I would say are my
weakest areas, I have shown growth over the last few years. By
looking at it that way, you know—comparing later performance to
the earlier performance, it sure feels better and more positive that
comparing your performance to others who may really be gifted in
those areas."

As that session came to a close, I began preparing Susan for
concluding therapy and continuing her future growth on her own.
Recognizing that many patients who demonstrate the kind of
growth that Susan did are reluctant to discontinue therapy, I
approached the subject gradually and cautiously. "Susan," I asked,
"When can you start running a support group for people wishing to
better understand and improve self-esteem?"

She smiled as she responded, "Do you need some help in the
office?"

After a brief pause, I shared, "Well, I could probably always use
help in the office; but, I was thinking more about people in your
local church or women's ministry group. I really think that you
have gained a handle on this thing; although I know you will keep
working at it over the months and even years to come, I think you
have turned the corner so to speak ... you are ready to launch out
there on your own!." I continued by saying, "Why don't you and
your husband review the goals you had as we began therapy; and, in
your next session we can evaluate your progress and insure that we
have addressed and either resolved or certainly gained insight on
how to resolve those issues."

As had become customary, Susan and her husband were a few
minutes early for their next session; they shared that they enjoyed
the time waiting in the waiting room where they could enjoy the
peace and quiet while listening to the calming music. Although

excited about reporting their discussion had confirmed that the initial goals for treatment had been met successfully, Susan shared her concern that she didn't want to stop the sessions altogether as she felt they had helped her so much. I concurred with her reluctance to terminate sessions as a normal feeling of patients showing as much growth as she had experienced; I shared that I would also miss working with them as I complimented them for their investment in treatment and indicated that therapists find it much more exciting and rewarding to work with such motivated and sincere patients who make progress so rapidly. Although indicating to Susan that I really didn't feel she would need further professional support, I reassured her that I would be available should she begin to relapse or begin to re-experience symptoms. We closed the session with prayer, asking God to continue to bless this fine couple and their children, to reassure Susan during times of self-doubt, and to help her remain strong as she endeavored with her husband to become a more active part of ministry within their local church.

Chapter 6

Solutions For Dealing With Guilt

Perhaps one of the most powerful tools used by Satan to discourage and immobilize a person from recovery of past trauma or inappropriate decision making in their life is the emotion of guilt. Much like the concept of forgiveness, guilt is often misunderstood and sometimes conveyed by well meaning persons as conviction and a sign of unconfessed sin in one's life. While hidden or secret sin in one's life will and should produce a healthy sense of guilt and conviction, unresolved conflict will produce extreme discomfort that could be confused with guilt.

Most Christian therapists would accept the rationale utilized by Minirth and Meier in their book entitled *Happiness Is A Choice;* these psychiatrists suggest that guilt usually appears in one of two forms— "true guilt" and "false guilt."(1) They explain true guilt as an uncomfortable inner awareness that one has violated a moral law of God and the source of such guilt is from God. False guilt, on the other hand, is feeling guilty for something that in reality does not violate any of God's laws. While true guilt comes from the Holy Spirit's conviction on one's life and can lead to remorse and seeking forgiveness for wrong doing, false guilt is an artificial feeling that comes from sources other than God such as other people who attempt to influence one through what has become known popularly as "guilt tripping". Both forms of guilt can cause a multitude of emotional problems—but the resolution of each form of guilt is very different. True guilt requires that a person experience a sense of remorse, seek forgiveness, and allow Christ's shed blood to cover whatever the wrong that caused this feeling of guilt. After forgiveness, God justifies the person He has forgiven; and, according to Micah 7:19, such sins are cast or hurled into "the depths of the sea" or so removed from the sinner that they are never to be remembered again. The prophet Jeremiah describes it like this, "For I will forgive their wickedness and will remember their sins no more" (Jeremiah 31:34). False guilt, on the other hand, does not require forgiveness for there has not been any violation of God's law; instead, further understanding of their discomfort and the sources of such feelings can help to reach resolution and prevent reoccurrence of such feelings in the future. Experts who have studied this concept from both a biblical and clinical perspective have concluded as much as 70-75% of what Christian people think may be feelings of guilt, may actually be "false" guilt rather than the guilt that results from God's conviction on their lives.

If Satan can overwhelm the new Christian with confusion about his or her feelings, he can immobilize that person from any further growth; in many such cases, such discouragement results in the new convert giving up and returning to their old ways, thinking that following Christ is too difficult or beyond their reach. Satan works hard at convincing the new convert that the pangs of guilt over past deeds will remain despite the forgiveness that God has extended to them. It is important to help the new Christian accept God's forgiveness of their sins and help them understand that although they will remember their past deeds, the shed blood of Christ has covered the sins. It is unfortunate that people will not forget past sins; our minds are not capable of deleting past memories. The best we can do when memories of past sins are triggered is to remind ourselves that God has forgiven those sins; scripture confirms that he has blotted them out and that God "will remember 'these' sins no more" (Jeremiah 31:34). Memory of past deeds does not imply they are not forgiven; however, many new converts struggle with confusing the memories of their past with guilt or conviction from the Holy Spirit. Obviously, if the sins have not been repeated since forgiveness and there has truly been a change of behavior, then the forgiven sinner can claim victory over this guilt in his or her past life.

Just as it is important to understand the differences between true guilt and false guilt, it is equally important to understand the defensive nature of people. It is a natural human tendency to minimize or ignore things that make one uncomfortable—thereby de-sensitizing themselves to the urgings of their conscience and the Holy Spirit. Our predecessors often referred to this as "searing of the conscience." Through repeated minimizing and ignoring the promptings one has when compromising what he or she knows to be right, a gradual de-sensitization will take place. This process is rather subtle and most people are unaware it is happening; it usually goes unnoticed by significant others around them. Generally, it begins with a decrease in the time spent in personal devotions and regularly seeking the things that will enhance and promote holiness in one's life. One omission or compromise quite often leads to another; the process is a gradual but steady escalation as one begins re-prioritizing the values of his or her life. Time previously spent to enable and strengthen one's walk with God is replaced with hobbies, interests, or other activities that prevent sufficient time to live a disciplined life. While many of these activities are legitimate and not sinful in nature, they consume time that should be prioritized on spiritual matters.

The pain caused by true guilt when one truly begins to experience remorse for wrong doing can only be resolved by the shed blood of Christ and accepting forgiveness by God. Through gaining forgiveness, there can be a purging of any guilt associated with past deeds, thus becoming a spiritual healing, rather than merely feeling less emotional discomfort that can be achieved through the therapeutic techniques in counseling. Despite the excellent training and experiential background that has provided me expertise and confidence within my field, **I remain "awed" at the limits of mere application of these techniques in bringing healing from past sins that subsequently have produced guilt in one's life. Short of God's intervention, there is no healing! It is only through forgiveness that the overriding guilt can be purged, and thereby resolved.**

While achieving resolution of past guilt is often enhanced by the therapeutic techniques utilized in psychotherapy or counseling, there is no therapeutic technique that can successfully resolve guilt in this manner.

To receive this form of forgiveness from God, it is most important that the person who has sinned, or referenced in scripture as the "sinner", be truly remorseful and experience a sense of real guilt for the offense committed. Most important in this process of validating remorse is the total acceptance of responsibility for the offense. While circumstances or others may have contributed in some manner to encourage or entice the decision to sin, the sinner must be truly remorseful and avoid rationalizing, minimizing or excusing his actions in any way. This thinking is contrary to what our contemporary philosophers attempt to promote in their more secular explanations that tend to minimize or excuse the offender due to his state of mind or environmental influences that hampered better decision making. Modern thinking tends to "excuse" rather than encourage acceptance of responsibility for one's actions or deeds.

What results in such thinking is the offender feels inconvenienced and perhaps shame for his decision making, thus excusing himself for his deed and not permitting the development of true remorse or a sense of guilt for the wrongdoing. Webster (1995) defines **guilt** as **"a feeling of responsibility or remorse for some offense or wrong … "** and **remorse** as **"deep and painful regret for wrongdoing; a deep sense of guilt and mental anguish for having done wrong."**(2) **Regret** is defined as **"to feel sorrow or remorse for an act, fault … "** (Webster, 1995). (3) Remorse is suggested as a synonym for regret; regret is suggested as a synonym for remorse. Remorse implies a sense of sorrow about events in the past, usually wrongs committed or errors made; regret implies a feeling of sorrow or disappointment for what has been done or in some cases not been done. Resolution of true guilt through forgiveness by God, can only result when and only when a person experiences true remorse. Furthermore, this type of forgiveness will significantly decrease future repetition of the same sin since the offender has accepted total responsibility for his acts or decisions.

After accomplishing this and receiving God's forgiveness, such a person is usually eager to establish safeguards and boundaries that will help to prevent a reoccurrence of the same.

An example of a case I treated several years ago illustrates these principles quite well. I will call his name Jon to protect the confidential nature of his story. Jon had been referred by a physician who was treating him for panic attacks. Although he had been employed for 15 years, Jon's anxiety levels recently had become so intense that he was forced to discontinue a job that he had learned to love. He presented in my office on the day of his scheduled appointment demonstrating the typical features of extreme anxiety and panic. As I heard Jon explain his situation, my heart went out to this young man of thirty-five. After giving him several minutes to explain what he felt to be his problem, I suggested he undergo a personality evaluation which was a general procedure used with new patients to help identify issues that could be causing the symptoms. This evaluation consisted of true and false questions known as the MMPI (Minnesota Multiphasic Personality Inventory).

Jon agreed to complete this questionnaire, and a return appointment was set to share the results from his evaluation. I agreed to have a telephone consultation with his physician and recommended that the two of us coordinate our treatment to better meet his emotional needs. Through the use of both psychotherapy and psychotropic medication to help control some of the symptoms he exhibited, I was confident that Jon's condition would improve. Jon left the office in a somewhat improved state as compared to when he arrived earlier, although still exhibiting desperation as he wondered if there was any hope for his current emotional state. He returned on the appointed day to review the findings of his personality evaluation and consider recommendations based on that assessment. On this day, Jon was extremely nervous with intense levels of anxiety—possibly exhibiting levels seen by individuals hospitalized for their own protection. He shared that his pain was so great that he had seriously contemplated suicide prior to coming for that appointment, thinking there would be no resolution of the conflict that caused such distress in his life.

As Jon began to share vividly the agonizing memories of past years, in desperation he said, "There's something I've never discussed with anyone about me ... because I've been so ashamed and felt so guilty about it!" With his voice trembling and on the verge of tears, Jon went on to explain that at the age of 12 he had been sexually abused by an 18-year-old male cousin. This had gone on for several years until he turned 18 and left home to get married. He further shared that following this trauma as an innocent child of 12; he subsequently had several sexual encounters with homosexual men over the last several years. Tearfully, he shared that although not feeling he was gay or a homosexual, he was troubled by what appeared to be a compulsive drive that compelled him during those years to seek affection and love from others inappropriately. Although a typical reactive pattern of sexual abuse victims, such behavior only resulted in more feelings of desperation, emptiness, and overwhelming guilt.

At this point, the focus of our therapy session changed as I presented to him the concept of gaining forgiveness and purging from past guilt which might then allow Jon to forgive himself and eventually let go of this deep seated and painful guilt he experienced. I explored with him his spirituality and he readily admitted there had been no place for religion in his life even though his parents had been churchgoers and had probably prayed for him a number of years. As a clinician, my plan was to finish the assessment and then return to this issue by closing the session in prayer. I began to share my clinical findings, but after only a brief time, Jon interrupted me and said, "Dr. Miller, could you tell me more about this forgiveness thing ... I think that might be something that can help me!"

After a simple explanation of God's saving grace and Jon's admission that he didn't know how to pray such a prayer, he agreed to repeat a simple prayer of confession after me. Within a few short minutes, a new countenance was revealed on Jon's face as a genuine peace and calmness became evident. Yes, Jon had confessed his sins and asked God to forgive him of the sins he had committed. While recognizing that his subsequent acting out sexually was perhaps a result of his own victimization, Jon didn't try to rationalize or minimize his actions in any manner. He accepted full responsibility for his past decisions and actions; he requested God's mercy and forgiveness. What occurred next is hard to describe as it was one of those experiences that one has to almost be there to fully comprehend the situation. Jon's emotional state radically changed with very obvious features of a more calm and peaceful demeanor and facial expression. He seemed less stressed, more relaxed, and most importantly more at peace with himself as we continued the session.

I encouraged him to find a good church home where his new found faith could mature. After some thought, I told him about a smaller holiness church in his community and a pastor who was a personal friend of mine and who I knew would extend warmth and fellowship to Jon and his wife. With each subsequent session, further growth was evidenced as Jon continued to blossom as a new Christian. After receiving Christ as his personal Savior, he began the process of disclosing these secrets to his wife, as well as to his parents from whom he had been alienated a number of years. As he returned to their home and shared his faith, he found his parents quite relieved that their prayers had not gone unanswered and that their dedication had finally been successful. Within days, Jon's remarkable recovery enabled him to return to work—first on a part time basis and subsequently back to a full time role. To his surprise, his wife forgave him and the couple began working on their marriage.

As I have often thought about Jon's case as well as others like his, **I am overwhelmed by the power of God's saving grace and not only its power to transform lives, but also provide healing for past traumas and hurts—but even more so the complete resolution it provides for guilt caused by sin.** I am reminded of some of my clinical training, which took place under a very secular psychiatrist—probably agnostic, at best. Though an expert in his field, he quoted many of the world's religions in our training experiences, seemingly as an attempt to convince himself of man's need for a spiritual encounter of some sort. With confidence he shared that as clinicians, we would never be able to treat or bring healing to anyone's life unless we were able to help them consider the spiritual part of themselves; he emphasized that man is a combination of mind, body, and soul and that most treatment approaches only emphasized the mind and body, totally neglecting the most important—the soul!

The Psalmist writes about it in Psalms 103, "Praise the Lord, Oh my soul ... Who forgives all your sins, who heals all your diseases, who redeems your life from the pit ... " Song writers have tried to describe the amazing healing nature of His shed blood as "... not just blood but precious blood ... For it washed the sin of man ... it heals my body, and it sets my spirit free ... " Now Jon experiences it! Praise God for His power to change lives and set the guilty free!

Chapter 7

The Importance of Balance
And Proper Priorities

S tan was a rather large framed, muscular young man of 28 years of age; although dressed in casual clothing, he owned and directed his own dry-wall construction company. Due to his reputation for high quality workmanship, his business had grown by leaps and bounds and perhaps much faster than he was prepared to handle. Sitting in my waiting room on a referral from the ER physician that had seen him the night before at one of the local hospitals, Stan was diagnosed with panic attacks due to excessive stress in his life. After being checked out in the Emergency Room and not finding anything physiologically that would explain the increased heart rate, shortness of breath, chest pains, and nausea that had prompted his wife to call 911, he was released with his promise to follow-up with a psychologist within the next day or two. Even though he had been rushed to the hospital the night before by squad for fear he was having a heart attack, Stan was on his cell phone and making arrangements with one of his employees while waiting for his session with me. Wearing two pagers on his belt as well as carrying a cell phone and an over-stuffed brief case, his appearance gave the impression of "over-load". Upon entering the waiting room area, I waited for him to finish his phone call and then introduced myself and invited him and his wife back to my office. Stan was married to a lovely young woman—Teresa, who was expecting their second child; she looked to be about 6 to 7 months into the pregnancy. From my initial assessment of this couple's functioning, it appeared that they loved each other and both seemed committed to their marriage.

After comfortably seated in my office, I asked them to describe the purpose of their meeting with me and to give further details about Stan's assessment in the ER last evening. From their description of his symptoms, it appeared that Stan was extremely too busy with his blossoming construction company. He admitted to working several hours per week, commenting, "People think when you are self-employed or own your own business that you can set your own hours ... what a farce that is! I set my own hours all right, but to make this business happen, it takes between 80 and 90 hours weekly."

In an attempt to support her husband, Teresa then commented, "But, he does come home for dinner each evening ... most of the time he then has to go back out to check on jobs ... but we have a little time together at dinner." When I asked about the week-end schedule, Stan admitted to keeping this same schedule pretty much seven days per week.

He clarified, "I think that once things settle down and I can hire a couple of guys as foremen, then my hours will become more regular."

To this comment, Teresa shared, "But, honey in all honesty, you have been saying that for several months now ... it just hasn't ever happened!"

Stan tried to explain that the construction industry is a very difficult area to find loyal and dedicated employees. He shared that there are several men who can do quality work, but alcoholism seems to be a norm; because of this characteristic of many of his employees, work attendance and turnover is a constant problem. Because his company has done high quality work, most of the general contractors around town had heard of Stan and started referring work to him. Desiring to maintain the quality of work, attempting to respond to the needs of his growing business, and maintaining his good reputation within the construction industry, he admitted he had over-extended himself to the point of physical and emotional exhaustion. Although his wife and son had continued to attend Sunday School and church at the local church in their neighborhood, Stan took this time to check on jobs and organize work sites for the coming week. He would try to meet his wife and four year old son at a restaurant at about noon on Sundays, but he would often get tied up on a job site or lose track of time and miss that time with his family.

Stan's typical day started at 5:00 AM. After a morning shower, he would dress and leave for his warehouse office building. While eating his breakfast, which consisted of a donut and two cups of coffee he had picked up on his way to work, he would get his phone messages and make all the job assignments to his men for that day. The day would routinely be busy with very little down time for Stan. He would try to catch a sandwich for lunch at a fast food restaurant in route between job sites, but occasionally wouldn't have time for that either so he would try to nibble on snack foods and pop from the snack machines in his warehouse building. Stan was defensive when questioned about how he felt these practices might be contributing adversely to his physical health. He reacted with some irritation saying, "I just don't know what I can do about it ... I can't find anyone I can trust with my business ... the jobs have to get done as we are under contracts to complete the work by a certain date ... I do always try to get a good meal for dinner even though I sometimes have to go back out to check on a job afterwards."

Guarding against appearing judgmental or critical in any way, I asked relevant questions about his symptoms as I completed the clinical history and other parts of Stan's initial evaluation. While appearing supportive to her husband, one could easily sense a level of frustration and loneliness in Teresa. Now in the final months of her pregnancy, she was stuck more at home with her 4 year old son. In an effort to partially compensate for his absence in the home, Stan frequently made quick phone calls to Teresa throughout the day as he traveled between job sites. Teresa said, "Dr. Miller, last night was probably a wake-up call for Stan ... he's been pushing it too hard and his body is trying to tell him he has to slow down ... I don't know what the answers are ... but I am really scared ... he just can't continue to work as hard as he has been working!" As she looked over at Stan with obvious love in her eyes for him and tearing up slightly she continued, "We just don't want to lose him … we love him and need him too much to let that happen!"

What happened with Stan is typical with many folks who are trying to make a living and develop a stable future for their family. He had over-extended himself; and, at the expense of his own health was pretty much covering all the bases—or at least the ones having to do with his rapidly growing and prospering company. While he had purchased a new car for his wife and provided her and his 4 year old son with all the luxuries available to make their lives comfortable, these toys and conveniences did not substitute for his presence. Furthermore, Stan absolutely needed a diversion from work; he could not focus on his work 18—20 hours out of every 24. He even shared during our initial session that although he went to bed by midnight each evening, his sleep was restless and disrupted; he figured he got an average of 4 hours sleep each day.

Stan, like a multitude of people today, had lost his sense of "balance". His schedule was erratic, it lacked consistency; he felt like he got nothing done but "putting out fires" and managing to keep all his men working and completing the jobs on time. Of course, then he had to deal with his accountant to ensure that payroll was done on time and that all the fiscal reports were completed by the required timelines. Even the time spent at home was quite often interrupted by phone calls from contractors or return calls that Stan hadn't been able to make from his cellular phone in between job sites. Even when he was home for an evening, Stan would sit down in the family room with his wife and son, but would be primarily focused on completing necessary paperwork for keeping the business on track or completing data reports for his tax accountant.

Stan was what many would refer to as "stressed out" or on "stress overload." What exactly is stress and at what point does it become stress overload? Most clinicians would differentiate stress into "positive stress" and "negative stress." Positive stress is that initial pressure one feels when facing a challenge or problem. This type of stress is not such a bad thing for it can help one concentrate, focus, perform, and often help one reach their peak efficiency. After meeting the challenge, then one can relax and enjoy their accomplishment. On the other hand, negative stress is when one stays geared up and fails to relax after meeting the challenge. Negative stress is when stress becomes a constant ongoing cycle, adversely affecting one's health and well being. Negative stress is linked with many physical ailments—tension headaches, high blood pressure, acne, nervousness, agitation, insomnia, lethargy or lack of energy, heart attacks, etc. Stress can stem from pleasant or positive events such as marriage, enlarging the family by childbirth or adoption, job promotion, move to a new home, etc. It can also stem from more negative or unpleasant events such as death of a loved one, marital conflict, required overtime work hours, challenges in parenting a strong-willed youngster or children experiencing medical problems, illness of family member, caring for aging parents, extended family conflicts, etc.

In the case of Stan, the initial excitement and stress around starting a business and seeing the rather instantaneous growth probably started as positive stress. This positive stress helped him concentrate on the organizational details of a young business and this quite likely helped him make it a successful and profitable company with an excellent reputation for quality work. However, when appropriate limits were not placed on time spent at the business, his time and focus on the other aspects of his life—family life, physical and emotional health, church and community involvement were sacrificed. Stress became a constant ongoing cycle without a realistic solution. He began spending less and less time with his wife and family, he stopped spending time in previously enjoyed hobbies or past-time activities, he and his wife had not had a date in several months despite having only been married for 7 years, he had stopped going to church and had even sacrificed the time previously spent in daily devotions and prayer. When asked why he had stopped doing these things, he responded with some frustration, "I really didn't want to stop doing these things and I do miss doing them now ... there just isn't any time to do them!"

As we brought his first session to a close, I detected some sense of relief from both Stan and Teresa as they had at least come to a better understanding of the problem. While we had not come to any conclusions or even discussed ways to help Stan with his dilemma, he seemed optimistic we would develop strategies to find a better balance for his life. He agreed that he must find a way to reduce the time and energy he spent in the business; he expressed a sincere desire to resume time spent in the other aspects of his life which he knew were very important. As he took his wife's hand, he shared, "I really want to get back to having our time together ... I miss the times we use to spend talking about our day ... I'm missing the exciting developments of our son ... I'm going to have to get these things under control within the next couple of months because I want to be there when our baby is born!"

Balance in our lives and maintaining proper priorities can help to prevent many problems resulting when such a balance is not kept. Despite our desire to follow proper priorities, the fast pace we maintain and the demanding society in which we live do not allow sufficient time for everything. Over commitment or excessive time spent in any particular area will prevent the balance that God has designed as proper. Ecclesiastes 3:1 admonishes, "There is a time for everything, and a season for every activity under heaven." Over-involvement in any area of our life, even legitimate things, can become the rationale and serve as an escape from obligations in important areas such as marriage, family life, employment, and work within our community and church.

Stan was not trying to escape from his obligations; the demands of running a business simply robbed him of the time and energy he really needed to provide in those other important areas of his life—especially family. He loved his wife and son very much; his dedication, commitment, and willingness to work hard at his business were made in an effort to provide financial stability for his family. While many of his peers worked merely a 40 hour per week job and literally spent multiple hours with their buddies in sporting events, hunting, or race cars, Stan had not even removed the canvas that covered his boat in the last six months. When asked why he hadn't gone boating recently, he replied, "I really use to love boating, but I wouldn't be able to take Teresa out right now with the pregnancy and I wouldn't want to take whatever little time I have with her and my boy away from them. I asked Stan if he would be willing to take on a small challenge sometime this next week-end. He responded affirmatively, "If I can do it." I reassured him that it would certainly be simple enough for him to accomplish and that Teresa would understand the two hours it would take.

I then described my challenge, "I want you to pick a two hour block of time, take your little boy with you to the garage, then I want you two guys to take the canvass off that boat and polish it up in preparation for a later trip to the local lake some Saturday afternoon."

"Well, I'll do it if you think this will help, but I'm really not sure why as I can't see where there will be an available Saturday afternoon for a boating excursion in the near future," Stan responded.

Teresa joined me in this plan by sharing with her husband, "That would give me two hours of needed rest and perhaps I can take a brief nap while you guys are spending time in the garage."

Stan reported in his next session that he had forced himself to do the challenge. He shared excitedly with a genuine smile, "I had forgotten how much enjoyment I use to get in just cleaning and preparing my boat for the water ... of course, my four year old assistant slowed me down some, but I can see the goal was not efficiency, but spending time in a father-son activity ... I really enjoyed it!"

Teresa then piped up, " ... and I got some much needed rest while they were in the garage ... it's so reassuring to a mother to see her child spending good quality time with his father ... I want our son to become just like his daddy!"

Over the weeks that followed, I continued to encourage Stan and Teresa to carve out little segments of time they could spend together as a couple or as a family. She started meeting him a couple of times per week for lunch at a local restaurant; on other days, she would prepare a simple picnic lunch and meet him at a worksite where the family would have a small picnic out of the trunk of her car. Despite the joking that he took from his men, Stan said he enjoyed meeting his family like this and that this might just be setting a good example for his men about the importance they should give to their families as well. Stan even turned some potential contracts down as he said he just didn't have the time or manpower to complete the jobs on time; while careful not to damage his reputation or the chance for future contracts, Stan became rather skillful in selecting the appropriate number of jobs that he could handle within a 6 day work week. At my suggestion, Stan decided to eliminate working on Sunday and make that a day with his family. Unless an emergency occurred, he avoided doing anything having to do with the business on Sunday. He returned to church attendance with his wife and son; they generally spent Sunday afternoon in some family activity and even took the boat out to the lake a few times for brief excursions which Teresa said she could handle just fine.

When encouraging Stan to return to church and re-institute the personal devotional time with God he had once had, I shared with him that I felt if He honored God in these things, God would help him solve some of the challenges he faced in his business. It's nice to feel you are right as a therapist, but even better when what you shared comes true! Stan and Teresa began meeting other couples and doing some fellowship in small group activities sponsored by their church. At one of these events, Stan and Teresa met a young man and his wife; this man had recently lost his job in a construction firm. After talking with him, Stan felt that although he hadn't worked within the drywall specialty field, his management and supervisory skills would easily transfer to that industry. After checking his references which were positive and getting a positive impression of this man and his wife from Teresa, he decided to offer him a job as one of two foremen he wanted to hire for the business. This man not only worked out well, Stan really enjoyed having a fellow believer work in his business as he could tell he was a man of integrity and deep commitment to God.

Stan became quite close with his new foreman; they were able to share on a more personal level as they had kindred spirits and values. When discovering that he also had his devotional time in the morning prior to coming to work, Stan suggested maybe they could meet together a couple days a week in the office for prayer and devotional sharing prior to starting the work day assignments.

The two men began sharing scripture verses that seemed to focus on allowing God to help manage the normal stressors in life. Some of the verses they shared at these times included the following:

- John 16:33 " … in me you may have peace … "
- John 14:1 "Let not your heart be troubled … "
- II Corinthians 1:8—12 speaks of being under great pressure; admonishing not to rely on oneself, but to rely upon God
- Phillipians 4:13 "I can do everything through Him who gives me strength"
- I Peter 5:6—7 "cast all your anxiety on Him … "
- John 14:27 "peace I leave with you … do not be afraid"
- II Timothy 1:7 " … God did not give me a spirit of timidity, but a spirit of power"
- Isaiah 40:31 "but those who hope in the Lord will renew their strength … "

They made it a matter of prayer to find an additional foreman that would fit within the structure they had developed and hopefully have a similar value system; Stan and his new assistant had become very good friends who shared each other's burdens and concerns. Within a short time, Stan shared that his new foreman had gotten a call from one of his former co-workers in the firm he had previously been employed and learned that another wave of layoffs had taken place, leaving this man without employment. An interview was set up for Stan to meet with this man; he was delighted to learn that he was a Christian in addition to having had a fairly good level of experience within the construction field. After their meeting and getting very positive references which included the man's pastor, Stan felt a similar feeling of confirmation to offer this man employment. However, prior to hiring him, Stan once again desired that Teresa meet this man and his wife as he had come to trust his wife's intuitive sense about important decisions like these. After confirmation by Teresa following a dinner meeting with the couple, Stan hired his second foreman for the business. Soon, this third man joined Stan and his first foreman for what became known as the "supervisory prayer & devotional meeting" that preceded the work days three times per week. Stan was then able to reduce his work load once again and now able to run the business within a 50 hour work week; he and his two foremen rotated being "on call" for emergencies and working 1/2 days on Saturdays with no one even permitted to work on Sundays any longer as this supervisory team wished to "model" the importance of Sunday being a day of rest and family time for their employees.

The initial steps employed with Stan to reduce his level of stress and begin to re-establish an appropriate balance within his life is what therapists would call "environmental manipulation". This practice includes assessing the environmental conditions and altering those things that are causing stress such as work schedules, excessive stimulation, insufficient time to relax, inadequate nutrition or sleep, and over-involvement in a particular activity even when a legitimate activity. There were of course other things necessary for Stan to successfully complete treatment and learn to manage the normal challenges of managing his business without compromising the other obligations he had to his wife, family, church, and himself. Although suggesting he consider appropriate medication that would help reduce or better manage his symptoms, he opted to avoid medication if at all possible. He expressed his commitment to try the environmental things first and if his symptoms didn't improve then consider medication. Several stress reduction techniques were shared with Stan; he was challenged to begin practicing some of these on a daily basis in an effort to help him gain some coping skills in managing normal daily stressors. These techniques follow:

1. Deep breathing: a simple technique that is basic to most other relaxation skills
   a. Inhale: sit or stand and place hands firmly and comfortably on your stomach, inhale slowly and deeply through nose, letting your stomach expand as much as possible
   b. Exhale: with hands on stomach, exhale slowly through your mouth, pursing your lips as if you

were going to whistle; as you exhale, stomach begins to feel flat

2. Clearing Your Mind
   a. allow yourself to mentally focus on a single, peaceful word, thought, or image—helps you take a mental and physical retreat from the "outside world"
3. Stretching
   a. Back Stretch: while sitting, stretch forward, rest your body on your lap, relax your head and neck
   b. Neck Stretch: while standing or sitting, slowly tilt your head to the right without moving shoulders, then slowly tilt your head to the left
   c. Shoulder & Arm Stretch: hold your hands together with fingers interlaced and stretch overhead with palms upward; hold for about 30 seconds, then relax
   d. Passive Back Stretch: lie on floor with your legs bent and resting on seat of chair, forming a 90 degree angle at knees and waist line
   e. Leg Stretch: with one foot on stool or support, lean forward; bend hips while keeping back straight
   f. Upper Body Stretch: with feet apart, reach overhead and stretch to the side
4. Progressive muscular relaxation
   a. Three step process: (1) tense a muscle, notice how it feels (2) release the muscle, notice how it feels (3) concentrate on the difference between the two feeling states
5. Visualization: a mental vacation; a "license to daydream"
   a. try to visualize yourself being warm, calm and relaxed
   b. picture a tranquil setting
   c. allow your memory to review a happy and relaxing event
6. Biofeedback: external sensors placed on body to measure specific stress responses such as perspiration,

temperature, and muscle tension
  a. stress cards give feedback by measuring the skin temperature
  b. blood pressure measurements also provide such feedback with stress reduction
7. Developing a Positive Attitude
  a. Positive Thinking: reframing or trying to interpret the situation in a more positive manner, the problem can become a challenge to solve rather than a crisis causing stress
  b. Adopting a new philosophy for life that says, "Problems are opportunities"
  c. Taking time to define the problem and breaking it down into smaller steps that can help resolve it rather than reacting or attacking the entire problem at once
  d. Self-Talk: telling yourself what you can and can't do
  e. Rehearsal: a way to prepare yourself for a potentially stressful situation by going over a plan in your mind

After Stan started getting a handle on his own stress management, he then began thinking of ways he could share these coping skills with his men and decided to begin scheduling some brief training sessions that would precede or follow the regular monthly meeting he had with them. In the first meeting he introduced the importance of keeping a balance in all activities and not even allowing work to interfere with time with family. Stan had asked me in one of his therapy sessions if I had any ideas he could share with his men and if there was a survey or small test they could take to help them determine their stress levels. I provided him with the following informal, self-administered Stress Survey (1) that could be easily completed, scored and interpreted:

Stress Survey

Directions: Rate each of the following items with the following code:
   Never = 0
   Once in a while (1 to 3 times per year) = 2
   A few times a week = 4
   Always or daily = 6

Questions:

1.   Do you eat on the run? _____
2.   Are you plagued by a rundown feeling and frequent illness? _____
3.   Are you too tired to exercise? _____
4.   Do you experience disrupted sleep, have difficulty getting to sleep, or staying asleep? _____
5.   Do you have difficulty saying "No"? _____
6.   Do you feel out of control of your life? _____
7.   Do you eat or drink or smoke when you are nervous, angry, or upset? _____
8.   Do you skip meals because you don't have time or in an effort to lose weight? _____

Your Score Means:

   0—10 points   Congratulations! You have healthy habits and are not stressed.
   11—25 points   You have average stress but the ability to cope with it
   26—48 points   You are experiencing a high level of stress and you need stress management skills

(Stress Survey adapted from Healthy Life Guide Pamphlet designed as a Promotional for Family & Psychological Services, Columbus, Oh, Jeanne Anselmo, RN, 1991)

Another resource Stan was provided in his therapy which he shared also with his employees in one of the training sessions was entitled **70 Great Stress Busters** (2) provided to our office by an advertising firm in New York by the name of Positive Promotions. A few of these suggestions follow:

- Make lists
- Eat right
- Take a deep breath
- Exercise
- Sing a song
- Call a friend
- Laugh at yourself
- Ask others to help
- Smile
- Take a deep breath
- Exercise
- Set realistic goals
- Take breaks
- Prioritize tasks
- Delegate work
- Avoid clutter
- Use proper lighting
- Have a hobby
- Keep noise down
- Talk things out
- Visualize a peaceful scene
- Learn to relax
- Budget time and money
- Plant a garden
- Massage tense muscles
- Reward yourself
- Go out for lunch
- Meditate
- Set limits
- Think positively
- Count to 10
- Enjoy small pleasure
- Avoid junk food
- Practice teamwork
- Believe in others
- Believe in yourself
- Confront your feelings
- Be kind
- Cry if necessary
- Remember: Time heals
- Get regular check-ups
- Take a walk
- Get organized
- Do neck rolls
- Avoid dangerous drugs
- Be flexible
- Stretch often
- Control your weight
- Avoid distractions
- Set reasonable deadlines
- Don't sweat the small stuff
- Learn to say no
- Forgive and forget
- Use the right tools
- Don't procrastinate
- Reflect on your joys
- Encourage others
- Get up earlier
- Break up monotony
- See problems as challenges
- Stop and smell the roses
- Love others
- Love yourself
- Avoid unnecessary meetings
- Screen your calls
- Give hugs
- Seek out positive people
- Be faithful
- Read good books
- Remember your triumphs
- Laugh often

Some of the workers became disgruntled when Stan and his two foremen had made an earlier decision to eliminate the option of working on Sundays; Stan explained their reasoning and said they were encouraging all their employees to spend that day with their families and hoped that part of the time would involve attending a church service of their choice. He also announced that he and the two foremen met on Monday, Wednesday, and Friday mornings for a brief time of devotional sharing and prayer prior to beginning the work day and that if any of the men would like to join them, they would be welcome. To Stan's surprise, a few of the men began coming to the devotional and prayer time; as time went along, additional men joined and it became a small accountability group which developed into quite an influential support mechanism for Stan and his employees.

Within several weeks of concentrated effort on Stan's part and some diligent re-organization of his commitments, he was able to "rebalance" things. He was able to discontinue therapy as his symptoms had diminished; and, he had learned several ways to manage the normal stress within his life. He had learned the importance of keeping a balance and had re-prioritized his priorities!

Chapter 8

Good Decision Making

Like other Christian counselors or therapists I deal with people almost everyday, sometimes hour after hour, who are dealing with the consequences and ramifications of poor decision-making in their lives. It never ceases to amaze me how seemingly intelligent and often quite religious persons can sometimes get themselves into real messes due to poor decision-making.

Such decisions include a multitude of issues that often contribute significantly toward producing stress in their lives. One very frequently occurring issue is the poor choice of a mate; statistics now suggest that all marriages only have about a 50% success rate. Unfortunately, these statistics have recently begun including people who are regular church attendees. Then there are the rather ominous poor spending and budgeting habits. It is not uncommon to see couples who have credit card balances up to $30,000 or more—balances that can't possibly be paid off through the payment plans offered by such banking companies. I will often see patients who are suffering from poor eating habits that have progressed into an eating disorder. Addictions of all kinds ranging from drugs/alcohol to internet and pornography are all too common even among folk who call themselves "Christian" and attend church on a regular basis. In recent months, I have seen a terrible increase in the number of both men as well as women addicted to internet chat rooms and pornographic sites.

Of course, occassionally there is reactionary decision making to stress, trauma, or hardships that have characterized one's life. Through no fault of their own, they may have been reared in a dysfunctional family or became the victim of trauma due to the sins of someone other than themselves. Quite often, perhaps all too often, I deal with problems that have resulted in one's life due to inadequate or insufficient boundaries in one's personal life or marriage thus resulting in poor decision-making.

Such is the case of Bill and Susan, a younger couple in their late thirties with two young teenage sons. Bill was the youth pastor of their church, which supplemented the income he earned from the full time position held with a major corporation in the city where they lived. Their early marriage had been somewhat troubled as Bill and Susan had come from rather different homes with little in common other than attending church. Having met in high school, they became high school sweethearts; they dated for about one year, and married soon after graduating from high school. They had started their family soon after marriage; Bill was taking classes part-time at a local university in hopes of completing his Bachelor's degree. Susan began struggling in her full time job with frequent absences due to deep depression manifesting itself in exhaustion and chronic fatigue, difficulty in concentration, generalized anxiety and agitation, frequent migraine headaches and insomnia. Although her physician had attempted treating these symptoms with medications in conjunction with psychotherapy, she continued to suffer, and was finally placed on disability by her employer.

The clinical picture is worsened by the extreme differences in their upbringing, which caused increasing stress for Susan, as she felt minimized and mistreated by Bill's family. Susan would frequently express deep hurt as she explained to Bill things his parents or married sisters would say to her at family reunions or celebrations. Rather than a happy time for her, holiday seasons would significantly increase Susan's stress and her symptoms would worsen as she anticipated the need to participate in such events as a part of the family. Although Bill claimed he had attempted to discuss these concerns with his parents and sisters from time to time, Susan shared none of these efforts were successful in changing the pattern that existed within the extended family dynamics. She tearfully expressed how she had prayed that God would change this pattern, as she really desired to have a closer relationship with her husband's family. She admitted to becoming so deeply hurt and frustrated with the situation that she had hoped they could move some distance from both their families in an effort to alter this pattern; but, recognized that such an option was not realistic and felt this would only be escaping the problem rather than solving it.

Perhaps this situation of strained family dynamics contributed to the poor decisions in spending habits that rapidly became a pattern in this young couple's lifestyle. Both Bill and Susan had come from middle class families and had been provided a good lifestyle growing up in homes that did not really have unmet needs. While growing up, both their parents had good incomes and provided well for their families. They both had grown accustomed to a comfortable life style without much practice in "delayed gratification" of one's desires. As with most young couples in today's society, they had become inundated with credit card solicitations with low introductory rates and promises of low payments for quick cash to get those things that advertisements made appear as "needs" rather than dreams or desires. Perhaps Bill was attempting to make his wife happier by purchasing things for the family, taking them out to dinner or on vacations they could not afford. They had sold their smaller home and purchased a larger one, feeling that since their application had been approved, it must be within God's will for them despite not examining closely the implications that an increased house payment would have on their monthly budget.

Despite what may have been positive efforts at bringing happiness to his wife and sons, Bill's leadership in financial management for the family had produced rather serious ramifications. At the time of starting therapy with me, they shared that they had discussed the various options in filing bankruptcy with an attorney, but indicated they were trying to delay that decision if possible as they feared what it would do to their credit. When asked details about their finances, Bill disclosed that aside from their house payment and two car lease payments, they owed over $90,000 in credit card debt. He admitted that most of this spending was not for tangible goods but resulted from eating out, getting cash advances to pay for vacations or week-end trips, or other consumptive activities such as attending hockey or baseball games with his sons.

Although having participated in psychotherapy two years before this time to address the unresolved family conflicts of the extended family, this re-initiation of therapy resulted when Susan called the office and requested an appointment due to what she described as the return of her deep depression. At this first session, Susan shared that she suspected her husband was involved in an affair outside their marriage; she tearfully described how he had changed. Bill had begun losing weight and purchased some new clothes for himself. She had discovered some credit card charges on their accounts that he avoided explaining to her. She conveyed that her husband now seemed more secretive and she suspected he was withholding information from her when she asked him about things. In an attempt to convince her that she just needed more responsibility for finances, he suggested that she get her own checking account and he could transfer money into this account each month for groceries and household expenses. The real crisis began when Susan found a charge at the local Hyatt Hotel on a night he had told her he was going to attend a hockey game with some co-workers. The charges consisted of both lodging and room service; his explanation to her changed slightly each time she asked him. She also felt his responses lacked substance and seemed to lack rationale or logic. Bill told his wife that he placed the room charges on his credit card as a favor to an employee of the company; he further assured her that this person was intending to pay him back. Further questioning by Susan only produced answers that made her more suspect of her husband's explanation. For almost two years, he had maintained this story without success in gaining back his wife's trust. Susan's intuitive sense caused her to begin having questions about her husband's integrity.

Although continuing to work in his church as an associate pastor and teaching an adult Sunday school class as well as preaching occasionally as such opportunities were given, Bill had maintained this story, which Susan felt strongly was a lie. Refusing to join his wife in therapy for several weeks, Bill maintained his story.

Finally in a crisis moment when Susan shared her intent to leave the marriage as she could not continue living with a man she couldn't trust, he agreed to attend a therapy session with her. Once again in that session, he conveyed the story he had maintained for two years despite Susan's confrontation of his inconsistent responses to her questions. But a few days later, guilt overcame his composure and he finally shared that his story was a lie. He began slowly disclosing the truth which took several days. Not only had Bill gone to the hockey game with a co-worker, but this co-worker had also hired two women to be their escorts. Bill still claimed that he never touched either of the women and didn't even flirt with them. Susan's continual questioning and pointing out the inconsistencies tended to erode away the validity of his story. Finally in desperation, he disclosed the graphic details of his adultery. He further offered explanation of another purchase that Susan had questioned which involved purchasing two tickets to the Ballet for his boss as a gift. When Bill's boss couldn't find anyone to attend with her, he volunteered. He rationalized that even though he realized it probably wasn't a good idea, "they were just going as friends" and that he "never had intended for anything further to occur."

Susan lashed out at her husband with justifiable anger; "You have never asked me to go to a Ballet! You had a date with your boss ... you weren't going as friends ... How can I ever trust you again?"

The days that followed were extremely difficult for both Susan and Bill. Susan shared that her emotions vacillated from deep sadness, hurt and depression to extreme anger. Bill met with Susan's parents and confessed his wrong and asked them to forgive him. He shared part of the situation with his two teenage sons who reacted with great disappointment. They were deeply troubled to discover that their father was not the man of integrity they previously thought he was. Their respect for him as their father and youth pastor was severely challenged as they pointed out to him that these decisions did not reflect what he tried to teach them and the other teenagers in their youth group. Bill also met with his pastor to confess that his explanation to him had been based on lies and that he was coming completely clean regardless of the ramifications it meant for his ministry or position in the church. He conveyed that being in the right relationship with God and his family was more important to him than his reputation at this time.

Why had Bill slipped into poor decision-making? Previously advising others and modeling for them the importance of keeping one's life focused on God and making decisions only that would be within God's will, Bill had radically lost his way! As we reviewed when the problem had started, he admitted beginning to compromise several months prior to the decision to attend the hockey game with his co-worker and the female escorts or attending the Ballet with his female boss. Through a review of several of his decisions he could see that one poor decision had led to another; and thus, there was a progression and cyclic nature to his poor judgments. The additional purchases that their budget could not afford resulted in his need to get a part-time job which decreased the time he had available to spend with family and cultivate his own spiritual life. Bill admitted that his personal devotions had been one of the first activities to be significantly decreased, as he explained, "I just didn't seem to have time." Recognizing he was less available to his sons and wife, he had tried to substitute his time with material things. Credit cards made such purchases possible; although Bill said he could see the pattern was getting worse and worse, he would try convincing himself that somehow he would turn it around and they could get back to living within their means.

Bill shared that he just didn't feel it would ever happen to him— "after all I had grown up in the church ... I was the youth pastor ... I taught an adult Sunday School class ... I advised others about spiritual matters ... I was a spiritual leader to others." Although some who find themselves in such a dilemma wish to blame God for allowing them to stray despite their "good works" within the church or ministry, Bill took total responsibility for his guilt. He admitted that he had sinned against God, his wife and family, and even himself.

Absolutely no one is invulnerable to poor decision-making; I have treated and continue to treat all levels of people including people who are a part of holiness denominations, college graduates of bible colleges, people who fulfill leadership roles in their church, and even ordained ministers from time to time. Perhaps our ultimate dependence upon God has been described best by a statement heard frequently in sermons addressing this area of temptation and compromise, "When we think we have become invulnerable to something, we are no doubt the most vulnerable!"

Patients often ask me how one goes about making good, healthy decisions; they seem to want a formula or technique that will increase their ability to make better decisions and therefore avoid repeating the pattern that has produced the current stress. Although there are a multitude of theories in the field and literally thousands of self-help books now available on this subject, I usually share an example from my childhood, which illustrates the importance of seeking God's direction in decision making.

My father, a Nazarene pastor, had ministered in the same church for a number of years; he had had a good ministry, successfully leading the congregation through a major relocation and building expansion program. Upon being offered an opportunity to consider a larger church by the District Superintendent, I remember asking him if we were going to move. To my surprise, his response was that he was praying about it. In my youthful, immature thinking, I said to him, "Dad, it's a bigger church ... it's more salary ... you know it's got to be God's will!" I was anxious to start packing!

With fatherly wisdom, he used this opportunity to teach me about "testing the spirits" and to fully examine all the issues, prayerfully seeking God's confirmation prior to deciding any direction. My father ended up not taking the church because as he explained it to me, he did not get confirmation from God to take such an option. He completed his commitment to this church and then later accepted a call to a smaller congregation where he felt God's confirmation on that opportunity. As my father did at this early time in my life, I try to direct my patients to I John 4 where we read, **"Dear friends, do not believe every spirit, but test the spirits to see whether they are from God, because many false prophets have gone out into the world."**

The next logical question becomes, how does one test the spirits? I would propose the following criteria for "testing the spirits" in decision making:

(1) **Slow down the decision making process:** Good decisions are usually not "micro-wave" decisions; they are the result of carefully examining the issues and prayerfully seeking God's direction as we weigh out the consequences and ramifications of each possible alternative. Despite living in a society that promotes "quick fixes" and impulsive decision-making, we increase our success by resisting societal standards and what might be seen as usual practices.

(2) **Pray about all major decisions:** God judges a heart of willingness, not the time it takes for us to make a decision; we need to pray that God will give us objectivity and insight rather than relying on our emotional response to something. An emotional, reactive response is often not wise and leads to unfortunate consequences that cause subsequent stress. Emotions are not always logical; decisions should be based on logic and rationale rather than emotion. In Luke 6:12 we see that Jesus **"went out into the mountains to pray, and prayed all night"** prior to making his decision on selecting his 12 disciples.

(3) **Think about and meditate on the issue and possible solutions:** Christians need to contemplate decisions by weighing out the advantages and disadvantages of all the possible options. If more time is taken at this stage, implementation of the decision is much less work and can be done more efficiently. **James 1:5 says that God will give a generous supply of wisdom to all who ask him.**

(4) **Consult with those whom you trust and respect as peers and spiritual leaders who you know can hear from God:** An objective viewpoint from others whom you trust can help to validate or invalidate possible directions you are considering. **Proverbs 12:15 describes a wise man as one who "listens to advice."** While consulting with others, be cautious to avoid those who try to tell you what God has told them is His

will for you. It has been my experience that God usually will speak directly to you in most cases! Others might validate it for you, but God usually speaks directly to the person who is sincerely seeking after Him and His will.

(5) **Avoid relying too heavily upon others for account-ability:** While it is wise to seek and listen to the advice of others, there is the risk of relying too heavily upon their input or what has become a popular notion among Christian circles as seeking approval from their "accountability groups." Good accountability groups can be a helpful resource and support for decision making; however, ultimately we are responsible to God and must represent our own accountability. Romans 3:19 clearly conveys that **we are ultimately "held accountable to God."** I often deal with people whose accountability groups have failed to keep them from sin. A few years ago I dealt with the ramifications of a very inappropriate decision of a small group of youth pastors who decided to visit a nude bar in a major city so they could allegedly "learn more about such a temptation as they felt it might enhance their ministry to the youth in their congregations." They rationalized they would go together and keep each other accountable. Clinically speaking, this is <u>not</u> an example of "accountability" but the opposite— "enabling". Instead of flirting with sin and temptation, we must flee and avoid it!

(6) **Look for validating or invalidating "signs" that help to confirm the decision:** Avoid seeking signs that will appear to be supportive of a desirable direc-tion, but sincerely and objectively weigh out any such sign to validate its authenticity. I recently had a man tell me that God had sent a woman into his life since God knew he was in an unhappy marriage and God wanted him to be happy. He referred to this as a "sign" –"a gift from God." I promptly informed him

that what he was calling a "sign" was adultery and clearly against God's Word. God never will utilize anything as a sign that is contrary to or inconsistent with scripture. People sometimes see and even seek to see what they want to see as validating signs. Getting approval for financing on a new car or home that then causes budgetary problems in paying tithes and offerings regularly is not only a false sign that some would rationalize is God's will, it isn't even good common sense.

But what about the decisions that others have made that adversely affect us? Quite often, we see people who have been traumatized by the ramifications of sin committed not by them, but by someone else. We live in a sinful world; scripture tells us that it "rains on the just and the unjust." Until Jesus returns and takes us to our heavenly home, we are all subject to the effects that sin has on this world in which we live. Sometimes it seems bearable ... other times not so bearable.

In such situations, I point my patients to 2 Corinthians 12:9, **" ... My grace is sufficient for you, for my power is made perfect in weakness."** During times of hardship and painful suffering, it's this grace that the Christian finds all so sufficient to maintain purity of heart, uphold a reputation of integrity, and remain steadfastly in the center of God's will! Despite feeling life is terribly unfair at such times since it is, this grace enables one to face whatever the circumstances and with God's help, successfully win the battle!

There is no clinical technique quite as powerful as this grace that God has and will provide to his children when they are injured or adversely affected by the sins of others. To persevere during these times will surely deepen our utter dependence on God; it also strengthens our walk with Him. The people I have the most faith and trust in—those spiritual leaders and mentors to me—have all faced adversity or trauma at sometime in their life. Though suffering pain or facing unfair circumstances caused by others, they chose to persevere. They chose to grow rather than become bitter. By utilizing God's grace and relying upon the sufficiency of this grace, they were capable of remaining faithful to Him.

And then there is the reward! God always rewards those who are faithful to Him! Words cannot describe adequately that "peace of mind" that results from knowing you have maintained Godliness in your life despite the circumstances that would entice other decisions. The reward isn't always as we would prescribe for ourselves or even on the same timetable that we might desire, but within God's timing, the faithful will be rewarded! **God will always reward your faithfulness to Him!**

In the story of Bill and Susan, Bill was a fortunate man! Despite the fact that God will always forgive one's sins and re-adopt him or her into the family, spouses who are deeply injured by unfaithfulness are not always able to re-build trust. Perhaps this is the reason God allows for divorce in such cases. Susan forgave her husband early on in the process, but it took months before she could confidently agree that she intended to stay with him and allow him to re-build the trust he had damaged so badly in his poor decision-making. Looking at him directly in one session, I informed Bill that his decision-making that led him to commit adultery had given his wife "biblical grounds" to divorce him. With a remorseful heart, he agreed and committed to whatever efforts it might take to save his marriage. Over the weeks and months that followed, Bill and Susan made significant changes in their home and marriage. After conferring with an attorney, they prayerfully came to the decision to file bankruptcy to correct the debt ratio they could never escape. They then established a reasonable budget that was based on their income without any reliance on credit cards. At the top of their list of weekly expenditures was "tithe" to their local church. Bill re-prioritized time with his family and placed appropriate boundaries on all relationships outside his marriage. Above all, Bill re-ordered his schedule to include adequate time for daily devotions and prayer.

How I wish all cases involving poor decision-making could end like Bill and Susan; but all too often they end in disaster.

Chapter 9

The Importance Of Learning How To Forgive

The patient was a young man who was employed as a Detective for the local City Police Division. He contacted me out of concern for his wife who was severely depressed and at times suicidal. She was pregnant with their second child, making the use of anti-depressant medication less viable. She had just discovered that her husband was involved in an affair with a bank teller where he was working a part-time second job.

This man had pretty much resigned himself to divorce, thinking that he had messed up his marriage so badly that his wife would never be willing to forgive him. I began working with his wife and made several outreach efforts to involve him in hopes that their marriage might be saved. Although reluctant at first, he finally agreed to meet with me, and I was able to involve them in joint marital sessions within a few weeks. During the course of treatment, he decided he needed a few days alone to think through on some of the issues involved and so he decided to go to South Carolina on a brief vacation. A few days later, we reached a very frightening juncture in the course of this couple's treatment.

It was at a very early hour one Saturday morning as I was preparing to see my patients for the day when the phone rang. I typically don't answer the phone on Saturday mornings as I am without secretarial coverage that day, and I attempt handling messages from the voice mail between sessions. But for some strange reason, I answered the call that morning. On the other end of the phone line I heard my patient's voice informing me that he was in a South Carolina motel room with a loaded gun and ready to take his life. He shared desperately how he felt he had hurt his wife so badly that she would never forgive him and he doubted he could ever forgive himself. He was informing me so that I might convey his remorse to her.

God has always provided the grace I've needed in such crises with patients; this incident was no different as I patiently directed him to the Gideon Bible in the nightstand next to the bed in that Days Inn. I encouraged him to read some scripture verses I referenced on forgiveness, among which was I John 1:9, "If we confess our sins, He is faithful and just to forgive us our sins and to purify us from all unrighteousness." I conveyed to him that God would forgive him, for it said so in the Bible. I further shared that I felt certain his wife wanted to forgive him since we had been discussing such issues in her sessions. Additionally, I tried to assure him, that together with God's help, he could over time forgive himself and possibly put their marriage back together. We finished our conversation and I went about seeing my patients for the day, frequently pausing to breathe a word of prayer that God would minister to this desperate man's heart through the scriptures he was reading. (*the rest of this story later*)

Why was it so hard for this man to accept that he could be forgiven by God, his wife, and that he could even reach a goal of forgiving himself for falling to this terrible sin? Thinking this was an impossible goal, he had concluded that his only option for ending the pain he had caused for his wife, family, and himself was to end his life in suicide. Experts in the field of mental health usually agree that among the various anxieties people experience is an unchangeable past. If they were completely honest, most people will share that they have regrets over earlier decisions they have made and wish they could change the outcomes they now experience from such choices. Many attempt to address such guilt over past deeds through psychotherapy and sharing with a therapist who can help them resolve feelings of failure over the past, and redirect energies toward the present and future decisions rather than "beat themselves up" over past behaviors that can never be changed.

Although there are not many studies on forgiveness available in the literature, the few that do exist suggest that forgiveness has been successfully used to help Vietnam veterans cope with post-traumatic stress disorder, survivors of suicide victims, physically disabled individuals, people living with HIV/AIDS, victims of domestic violence, substance abusers, the terminally ill, elderly patients coping with end-of-life issues, and at-risk adolescents who have experienced physical or emotional abuse. In 1998, ABC News reported that studies confirmed that forgiving or letting go of anger and resentment could reduce the severity of heart disease and that in some cases even prolong the lives of cancer patients.

While looking at forgiveness from a spiritual perspective can be quite different than from a clinical one, the two approaches are not incompatible—in fact, quite the contrary, they might be considered inseparable. Clinically, people present a host of symptoms that cause pain in their lives, and to some degree may somewhat disable them emotionally. Mental health practitioners attempt to discover the underlying problems that need resolution and healing; and thus, by addressing the root cause and hopefully resolving that problem, the symptoms will dissipate. Additionally, experts in the field continue to search for techniques or procedures that will decrease the pain or presenting symptom. As with the studies referenced above, they view forgiveness as a technique much like other procedures utilized within medicine. Forgiveness is not a technique—but rather an initial decision, which then becomes a process. We decide to forgive someone. This initial decision to forgive begins to form the foundation upon which we then allow the process of forgiveness to take place and thus bring healing that only God can provide through His infinite grace. Much like sanctification is for the believer, there is an initial forgiveness which involves a decision to forgive the offender; then secondly, the process of working through the issues and finally reaching a resolution to the matter. Within the holiness denominations, sanctification is sometimes explained as a two-step process: (1) the "crisis experience" or the conscious decision to totally surrender one's life to Christ and his service, and (2) progressive sanctification, which refers to the ongoing process of becoming more like Christ through spiritual maturation. Successfully reaching forgiveness may well resemble a similar process to sanctification—the second work of grace. Perhaps we could conceptualize the decision as "initial forgiveness" and the process as "progressive forgiveness."

Unfortunately, at times the church and well-meaning persons attempting to explain this concept have added more confusion than clarity. Multitudes of Christians hide the pain and trauma behind a superficial smile simply because they have not been able to reach resolution of offenses that were directed at them. For some, they are not refusing forgiveness, they just misunderstand it, and so they struggle with feelings of defeat. They pray desperately that God will help them to forgive the offender, only to be left with feelings of frustration and lack of resolution. For others, unfortunately, they have chosen to not forgive which takes them down a very destructive path of anger that if not resolved, ultimately leads to bitterness. This bitterness soon takes root and begins to grow, affecting other areas of their life and relationships with others as well as God. Holding onto unresolved anger can produce a bitter spirit and will usually lead to unhappiness and a lack of peace. Such bitterness can lead to a defeated spirit and certainly inhibit one's ability to reflect Christ in his or her life. Lack of forgiveness can be fertile ground for Satan's ongoing attacks and vulnerability to temptation. When past hurts are not let go, the individual appears more susceptible for further hurt since they are more likely to misunderstand or misinterpret situations that occur in their lives.

If confusion about forgiveness exists, then perhaps we should examine this concept closer by first of all defining it in practical terminology, then clarifying some of the misperceptions people have about this very critical issue in the life of a Christian. Webster's Dictionary (1996) offers a good definition of forgiveness (1), "to pardon an offense or offender; to cease to feel resentment against ... to give up resentment against or the desire to punish." Speaking on this subject in a sermon (2) at Circleville's Mt. Of Praise Camp Meeting one year, Dr. Marlin Hotle stated that the original Greek words used in scripture for forgiveness are consistent with Webster's definition since they mean, "to let go". In forgiveness, we must essentially let go of the resentment we hold toward that person who offended us. This is a decision one makes! If resolution is forthcoming, this decision must be made—there is no option! Scripture clearly commands us to forgive others, "For if you forgive men when they sin against you, your heavenly Father will also forgive you ... But if you do not forgive men their sins, your Father will not forgive your sins (Matthew 6:14-15).

The misperceptions about forgiveness are many times the result of being misguided by those well meaning people who have attempted to help resolve deep hurts or traumas without fully understanding forgiveness themselves. Statements such as "just give it to God" or "it sounds like you haven't committed it to God ... just surrender it and move on" or "you really haven't forgiven that person since you keep bringing it up ... " are not helpful for the person who is struggling to work through forgiveness. Such statements add further confusion rather than clarity. Many of my patients struggling with this issue have shared they have been made to feel guilty from sermons they have heard or books they have read that true forgiveness is dying out to any anger about the offense. Anger is an appropriate and normal response to being hurt by others; anger is merely an emotion like other human emotions we experience. What becomes critical is how the anger is dealt with or what it leads to if not resolved. Some have even expressed they struggle to think that they must approach the one who offended them, offering a generic apology in an effort to reconcile with the person guilty of the offense—otherwise they would not be "demonstrating a spirit of forgiveness". While this may be required or helpful in some situations, it is certainly not appropriate in all, and in certain circumstances would absolutely not be appropriate for to do so would only serve to enable the offender and allow them to further justify their act or offense. Obviously, if the offended person retaliated in some way or vented their hurts through unjust gossip to others in an effort to "get even" with the offender, then asking that person's forgiveness would be necessary to fully gain the benefits offered in the process of forgiveness.

Although preaching about forgiveness from a spiritual perspective, Dr. Hotle's sermon was the most clinically sound explanation on this issue I have ever heard. First on all, forgiveness is something that the offended or the victim does; forgiveness benefits "the offended" far more than it does "the offender". If by forgiving someone, you are "giving it up to God" or "releasing it"—you are simply deciding to not permit the hurt and memory of the offense to continue to affect you. Holding onto resentment and anger never hurts the offender—but it has a crippling effect on that person who possesses it. The resentful person does not possess the peace and joy that God wishes for His children to experience. Choosing to forgive someone does not mean that you are excusing the offense or saying it was acceptable; no, it simply means you are releasing it to God. By releasing the resentment held within the heart, one "frees" their mind to dwell on other matters of a more positive and uplifting nature. Dr. Hotle suggested that forgiveness is something one does for himself, and many times merely within himself.

Some people confuse forgiveness with forgetting; they have come to believe that if they truly forgive an offense, they will be capable of completely forgetting it. Through perhaps false teaching from their church or other sources, many people have come to the conclusion that we are to forgive others in the same manner that God forgives—which is just not possible. While we are to pursue a life that reflects Christ as our model, our humanness falls short of His divine characteristics. Scripture tells us that God forgives and casts our sins in the sea of forgetfulness, never to be remembered again. However, this is a divine attribute that we do not have; I use the analogy with my patients that our mind is like a very powerful computer that has no "delete" option. Whatever happens to us is recorded forever in our brain's memory; we do not have the capacity to eliminate it. We can decide to resolve it and file it away so to prevent it from causing further distress regularly, but the memory of it will remain in one form or another until we receive our heavenly body and God wipes away our tears for the last time. While we are not to "harbor" it by thinking about it frequently or replaying the scenario over in our minds, we cannot forget it as God does our sins. Because one does not forget an offense does not mean he or she hasn't forgiven the offender; **forgiveness is not synonymous with forgetting.**

Just as forgiveness does not allow one to forget the deep hurt or pain as a result of the offense, **forgiveness will not change the natural consequences of the act**. Sin has always had and always will have consequences! Galations 6:7-8 clearly conveys "a man reaps what he sows ... one who sows to please his sinful nature, from that nature will reap destruction ... ." All decisions lead to consequences, and while God can forgive the homosexual, he may still die from HIV or other diseases as a result of that lifestyle. The one who abuses his body with cigarettes can be delivered from the sinful addiction, but he may still struggle with emphysema or may even die from lung cancer. God can forgive the man or woman who commits adultery, but their marriage may still result in divorce. Although forgiven and now pure in the eyes of God, the consequences of their prior sins may still provide extremely difficult challenges as they struggle to regain the respect of friends and family members.

As discussed earlier, anger is a natural and quite logical emotional response to being offended. **Forgiveness is not the absence of anger**. While the Christian must let go of the anger or resentment he initially feels as a normal response to being offended, he can and quite likely needs to experience anger during the process of forgiveness. Ephesians 4:26-27 admonishes "in your anger, do not sin ... do not let the sun go down while you are still angry ... do not give the devil a foothold." By choosing to forgive the offender, the anger can begin to dissipate, and thus not lead to bitterness. Even after forgiving the offender, certain events or situations may cause the mind to once again re-experience the memory of the offense. These brief memories of the original hurt or offense are the result of what psychologists call "trigger" memories, when a memory is triggered, the individual quite likely will re-experience the emotional responses that characterized that original event. Since anger is one of those emotions, the individual might re-experience anger when that memory occurs; such an emotional response might cause the person to begin doubting if they have truly forgiven the person who offended them. When one understands the nature of trigger memories and the effect they can have on individuals after they have resolved past hurts through forgiveness, it is easier to simply renew the process of "releasing it to God" and once again file it away in what might be referenced as "closed files" of the mind.

Having worked with multitudes of patients struggling with this issue of forgiveness, I would like to propose a practical application that involves three steps: (1) **a definite choice or decision to forgive;** (2) **a change in behavior that begins the process of forgiveness; and** (3) **a renewing of the mind by consciously letting it go and focusing on other things**. Hebrews 12:14 commands us to "make every effort to live in peace with all men and to be holy" since "without holiness no one will see the Lord." This verse very clearly tells us that we have no option but to forgive others—for to fail in this command, we fail to achieve holiness, and without holiness we will never see God! Other scripture, such as Ephesians 4:31, further validates this same command; "Get rid of all bitterness, rage and anger, brawling and slander, along with every form of malice."

The Christian has no option but to make the **decision to forgive**; postponement or forfeiting forgiveness ultimately will lead to bitterness, which becomes to the spiritual body (psyche and soul) much like a cancer that eventually destroys the human body and normal functioning. Clinically, there seems to be a natural progression in choosing to not forgive a wrong; ill feeling toward that person leads to a rejection of him or her, and then comes the beginning seeds of bitterness, which take root and quickly mature into an unresolved anger. The unresolved anger is enhanced with brawling and slanderous efforts to further justify the decision to not forgive. One usually justifies this by saying the wrong is unforgivable; the person committing the wrong does not deserve forgiveness. Over the course of time, this initial seed of bitterness becomes an all out rage that manifests itself in various forms of behavior and emotions, in a variety of settings, and with a multiple number of persons other than the offender initially responsible for the wrong.

On the other hand, one's choice to forgive will lead to a **change in behavior**! Rather than finding ways to justify the bitterness and ill feeling toward the offender, one chooses to act in a forgiving manner and fulfill what Ephesians 4:32 suggests, "Be kind and compassionate to one another, forgiving each other, just as in Christ God forgave you." This is not an easy process, for it means one has chosen to take the first step in making a conscious decision to forgive the wrong. This second step will help to validate the first step; one's actions speak louder than words in demonstrating that the decision to forgive has been made. These actions are not easily accomplished for the process of forgiveness has only begun. Such action steps are taken despite the human nature that would suggest the offender is not worthy of such forgiveness. Romans 12:19-21 may provide some help in this process, "Do not take revenge, my friends, but leave room for God's wrath, for it is written: It is mine to avenge; I will repay, says the Lord ... On the contrary ... If your enemy is hungry, feed him; if he is thirsty, give him something to drink ... In doing this, you will heap burning coals on his head ... do not be overcome by evil, but overcome evil with good." This becomes quite a challenge to accomplish, for the human nature in us has a natural inclination to repay evil with a neutral response or no response at all—even for the sanctified Christian. The sanctified Christian, though fully committed to God and free of the carnal nature, still has a human nature, which will only change when receiving the new spiritual body in heaven. It's not human nature to respond to evil with kindness; this can only be accomplished by depending upon God's grace and consciously taking efforts to do so against emotions that would suggest a different response. Perhaps this type of response only becomes easier with the sanctified person for it requires a complete surrender of the self to God and the eradication of the sin nature or natural sin. I tell my patients to think of it as "taking the high road;" rather than stooping to the level of the offender with your response, "Respond as Christ would respond." When responding in this manner, people can look at themselves in the mirror and feel good about who they are and the "Christ-like-ness" they see rather than an image of revenge or a "get-even" spirit that results from an attitude of retaliation.

Having accomplished the first two steps in this practical application of forgiveness, efforts are then directed toward the third—**renewing of the mind**. The mind is a very powerful thing—it is the master computer of the entire body; it is far more powerful than some of the largest computers in the world. Experts in the field of cognition and brain anatomy tell us that the average person only utilizes a very small portion of the brain's potential and only a fraction of the billions of brain cells available. While this computer doesn't have a delete button and all memories—especially those of a traumatic nature—will always remain in our memory bank in some form, we can take control of our mind and decide how such memories will be filed by choosing to forgive and resolve such issues. Paul gives sound advice for taking control of the mind in Philippians 3:12-14, "Not that I have already obtained all this, or have already been made perfect, but I press on to take hold of that for which Christ Jesus took hold of me ... But one thing I do: Forgetting what is behind and straining toward what is ahead, I press on toward the goal to win the prize for which God has called me heavenward in Christ Jesus." Here, Paul transparently admits the difficulty in accomplishing this level of behavior, but yet a definite decision to do so with God's help. Though difficult and sometimes seemingly impossible to accomplish within ourselves, one must decide to put offenses behind them and STOP thinking about them by refocusing on other more important things—"pressing forward and thinking heavenward." Paul rightly describes it as a choice ("but one thing I do: forgetting what is behind") and with much difficulty and hard work (" ... and straining toward what is ahead").

I challenge my patients struggling with such a forgiving response to think in terms of how Christ would respond to such offenses. Scripture has a wealth of examples of how Christ responded with love to situations where others might have retaliated or responded with hostility. If our prayer each morning is to be more like Christ and for our lives to reflect Christ as a testimony to others, we help to prepare a "mindset" or establish such an attitude that makes this challenge much easier to accomplish.

In the therapy office, psychologists may utilize a number of techniques to help people work through the process of forgiveness. At times we have people write letters as a means to help them externalize their feelings and help them understand the dynamics behind their pain. Frequently, while reviewing the contents of such letters during the editing process, one can begin purging the inappropriate emotions that have become associated with the offense or offender. Though very seldom ever sent to the addressee, this process can be a helpful means of identifying and clarifying the specific issues requiring forgiveness, which are sometimes insights that make the process of forgiving that offender much easier. At times, victims will actually stop feeling sorry for themselves and begin having pity on the offender as they gain insight as to why the offender acted in the manner in which he or she did. A similar approach, called "the empty chair" technique accomplishes the same results by having the victim talk their feelings out to the chair, which represents the person who offended them. Through the process of discussion, with the guidance and clarification provided by the psychologist, similar goals can be accomplished. Ultimately this choice to forgive is an individual one and controlled by the victim. Only when the person decides to let things go, and accept God's grace to help them forgive, can the final step of forgiveness be accomplished. *(the rest of the story)*

You'll remember the City's police detective contemplating suicide in the South Carolina motel room since he didn't feel forgiveness was possible in his case. As you might suspect, God did intervene; in his next appointment, my patient told me that he felt the verses he had read that day in the motel room certainly helped to change the course of his intentions. He smiled as he explained it had been a long time since he had read the Bible and it took a while for him to understand the meaning of the verses. He shared that the verses seemed to speak to him and began helping him feel some hope, despite the mess he had made of his life.

As I continued to work with this couple over the next few weeks, God began to work miracles in this man's life and a marriage that most clinicians would have given up as hopeless. They returned to church and began spending more time together in an effort to repair the damage that had occurred in the months before. They decided to save their marriage; he quit the second job and transferred shifts to enable them to spend more time together as a family.

I have followed this family over the past twelve years; as a Detective for the police division, I have on occasion found consulting with him on legal issues quite helpful. I recently had such an opportunity. After we discussed my case and the related issues for several minutes, he updated me on his family situation. From his discussion, I could tell he and his wife are doing well. They remain in love and loyal to each other. This proud father then gave a status report on all three of their children: their older son is now a young teenager, about ready to start driving; he shared how well his middle school daughter was doing; and then with some emotion in his voice, he paused before sharing about their youngest daughter who is now 8 1/2 years old. With emotion that one doesn't usually hear in the voice of a veteran detective, he shared "Dr. Miller, if it weren't for you, we wouldn't have our youngest child ... we wouldn't even be together as a family." I gently corrected him as I have done in previous conversations with them, pointing out that it wasn't me—but his decision in a South Carolina motel room to first of all accept God's forgiveness of his sin, then to accept his wife's forgiveness, and finally to work through forgiving himself of the terrible choices he had made in his life. Their hard work as a couple, combined with God's healing, and the willingness to forgive each other and themselves produced a peace and joy out of what would have ended in disaster.

Chapter 10

Perfectionism—
Is It An Emotional Problem Or
A Sign Of Holiness?

U nlike other patients that I've treated for anxiety or depressive symptoms who are usually older, Judy was a young teenage girl of only 14 years of age. She sat calmly in the waiting room while awaiting her appointment; but, while appearing calm on the outside, she experienced a ravishing storm of emotions on the inside. Her mother described her daughter to be suffering from a mixture of emotions ranging from depression to extreme anger and withdrawal from others; while she attended a Christian junior high school and the church that sponsored the school, she had few friends. To further complicate Judy's clinical picture, she had developed a nervous habit of picking at her skin. Obvious open sores were observed on both her arms; she admitted to also picking the skin at other parts of her body as well. This habit, which may have initiated as an innocent nervous behavior, had progressed to a full blown case of what clinicians refer to as obsessive compulsive disorder—an extremely serious and severe anxiety disorder. She felt rejected by her peers and shared that she didn't have many friends at school or church. Judy's mother explained that she felt her daughter was still struggling to some extent with anger directed at her father who had deserted the family about one year before. Although professing to be a Christian, this man apparently lived a "double" life as there were several things about him that neither Judy, her brother, or his wife knew about until after he left the home. To further complicate things for the family, the mother explained that they had lost their home since her husband had stopped making mortgage payments several months before. The bank had foreclosed on their home, forcing the family to move to a small apartment.

As I greeted Judy and her mother in my waiting room, I sensed an underlying fear on both their parts—while Judy seemed fearful of sharing her innermost pain with this strange man whom she didn't know, her mother seemed desperately fearful about finding relief for her daughter whose pain she was also experiencing as only a mother can do for her offspring. After comfortably seated in my office, I began gathering the relevant information about Judy's condition from both Judy and her mother. After a few minutes, Judy gradually relaxed somewhat and began sharing more openly about her pain. She indicated that she had started picking at her skin during baths or showers, while her skin was wet. She further shared that the amount of time she spent in the bathtub or shower had probably gotten longer since beginning this behavior; her mother validated this to be the case. Although previously a straight "A" student and obviously quite bright, Judy said she didn't ever feel good enough and that she could always do better—especially now that her grades had dropped to include a few "B"s. When asked about her father, she became more evasive and from the change in emotions combined with cues from non-verbal body language, one could easily detect repressed anger at the man for whom she had lost all respect and confidence. She admitted to being angry at her dad for what he did to the family and especially her mom. She further shared how she realized that her problem was further hurting her mother, but that she didn't know how to stop it. She said in desperation, "I tell myself that I just won't pick at my sores and I really mean it, but then I can't get the thoughts out of my mind unless I pick ... then after picking at the skin for a short while, at least I get some relief from these thoughts that are always there in my mind ... !"

Although generally using the first session to build rapport and a trusting relationship while gathering data about the patient's condition, I could tell that the desperation experienced by this young lady and her mother required immediate intervention. I quickly explained that I felt from the description of Judy's problem that she had developed Obsessive-Compulsive Disorder and that this condition would require both psychotherapy as well as medication to alter the thoughts and subsequent picking behaviors. While Judy and her mother viewed a brief video that explained the condition and the medication utilized to treat it, I quickly dictated a brief report that they could take with them to their family physician who would then prescribe the medication necessary to help manage these symptoms. I quickly answered their initial questions and gave them the assurance that I felt with God's help, combined with medication and therapy, that Judy could find relief from this condition. I scheduled the second appointment within the next few days and reminded them to get an appointment with her physician as soon as feasible as it would take some time for the medication to begin working.

What is this disorder referred to as Obsessive-Compulsive Disorder? Why aren't Christians protected from such problems if they remain faithful to God and genuinely ask Him to help them balance their lives and direct their paths? Hadn't Judy and her family suffered enough with the loss of her dad, their home, and now the financial hardship that characterized their day to day existence with a single income? Would Judy have this disorder the rest of her life or would she need to take medication the rest of her life to manage it? These were all very relevant questions that Judy and her mother had on that first day of her treatment.

Let's first of all look more comprehensively at Judy's condition. Experts in the fields of psychology and psychiatry define Obsessive Compulsive Disorder, or OCD for short, as an illness that traps people in seemingly endless cycles of repetitive thoughts that won't leave their minds (obsessions) and in feelings that they must repeat certain actions over and over (compulsions). While it is possible for people to only experience the obsessions without the subsequent compulsive actions, clinicians only find this in about 20% of the cases treated. In about 80% of patients treated for this condition, the obsessions are accompanied by the compulsive behaviors. In fact, the compulsive actions tend to relieve the anxiety caused by the unwanted and uncontrollable thoughts. Like Judy, many OCD patients say that they seem to get some relief from the obsessive thoughts only after completing the compulsive action that becomes associated with the thought. The obsessions or thoughts that are definitely unwanted by the person seem to intrude into the person's everyday thinking; they may be frightening, disgusting, painful, or trivial. Common obsessions include fear of germs, fear of harming a loved one, or constant doubt. Most persons with OCD realize that their obsessions don't make any sense and are often irrational, but they are not able to ignore or suppress them—no matter how hard they try. They may be able to explain in great detail what their obsessions are, but cannot explain why they have such thoughts or why they feel powerless in controlling them. These thoughts range from an occasional idea that crops up ever so often, or more typically, may be almost constant. While some thoughts may just be annoying, the thoughts experienced by a majority of OCD patients seem to cause a great deal of suffering and prevent the person from relaxing and enjoying life. Like Judy, most cases of OCD are considered a form of anxiety disorder as they may start with feelings of discomfort or dread but build to an uncontrollable and unbearable level of anxiety.

Common obsessions seen by clinicians treating this condition include a range of things including the following:

- Fear of getting dirty, contaminated, or infected by people or things in the environment
- Fear of AIDS or HIV
- Disgust over body wastes, secretions, or other bodily functions
- Concern that a task or assignment has been done poorly or incorrectly, despite knowing this is not the case
- Extreme concern with orderliness, symmetry, exactness, or being exact and perfect
- Fear of thinking evil or sinful thoughts that go against

one's religion; some even feel convinced they have committed the unpardonable sin
- Fear of losing important things that will be needed later
- Recurring thoughts about harming or killing others or oneself
- Fear of committing a crime, such as theft, burglary, or shoplifting
- Recurring thoughts or images of a sexual nature
- Extreme concern with certain sounds, images, words, numbers, or the way things are verbalized
- Fear of blurting out obscenities or insulting others in some way
- Fear that a natural disaster will occur for which the person will have no control

While obsessions are the irrational thoughts, compulsions serve to relieve the anxiety and involve some action that is taken to extreme, becoming irrational in nature. Most patients experiencing OCD feel they have to do something which tends to relieve the undesirable anxiety they feel over the thought. For the person experiencing the obsession of being contaminated or getting dirty, the compulsive behavior that serves to decrease this anxiety is usually hand washing or a related cleansing process such as extended and excessive numbers of showers or baths. OCD patients may wash their hands excessively to the point of their skin drying out and cracking; or they may check that the stove is turned off again and again and again. These feelings that they must repeat certain actions or rituals are their compulsions—the things they feel they must do to avoid some dreaded event or to prevent or undo some harm to themselves or others, as suggested by the obsessions they experience. It is not unusual to see the OCD patient performing the compulsive behavior according to certain rules. These certain rules become somewhat like a ritual for the person performing them; the ritual may be very simple and hardly noticeable, or it may be very elaborate. Some people who have only obsessions may engage in mental rituals and avoidance—thus others are unaware of the pain they hide so well. Rituals can be so time-consuming, sometimes taking hours to complete, that they interfere with the person's daily routine. Rituals do seem to lessen anxiety, discomfort, or feelings of disgust, but only for a brief time. As the fear and tensions soon return, the patient feels compelled to repeat the ritual again in hopes that he or she will get some relief from the thoughts that overwhelm their thinking.

Common compulsive behaviors or rituals are listed below:

- Cleaning and grooming behaviors such as washing hands, showering, and brushing teeth in particular ways
- Touching certain objects in a specific manner
- Repeatedly cleaning items in the house
- Ordering or arranging things in a certain way
- Checking locks, electrical outlets, light switches, or fuses repeatedly
- Repeatedly putting clothes on, then taking them off; being bothered by tags in the back of clothing items
- Repeating certain actions, such as going through a doorway or avoiding stepping on the cracks between sidewalks
- Counting over and over to a certain number
- Hoarding items such as old newspapers, mail, containers, etc.
- Checking to see that no one has been hurt or killed, or no other disaster has occurred because of something the person with OCD has done or neglected
- Constantly seeking approval of others (especially children)

Judy did not fit nicely into either the list of common obsessions or compulsions. After evaluating her condition in the initial session, I hypothesized that her obsessions might involve certain repetitive sinful or evil thoughts that were contradictory to her religious orientation. I reasoned that her skin picking compulsion might be serving as a self-punitive action for having the thoughts that she felt were evil or sinful. Perhaps by picking at her skin and causing some discomfort or pain, she felt vindicated for at least a brief period and her thoughts (or obsessions) would subside. At any rate, I seriously understood the crisis nature of her situation as she displayed open, seeping sores that were below at least two layers of skin. None of the sores had scabs formed over the opening, thus signaling to me that her picking at these sores was a continual action, never allowing even a scab to form over the opening to promote healing. Like many OCD patients, Judy would need to begin discovering through psychotherapy the sources of her pain and attempt resolution of those conflicts in order that she might gain some control over both the obsessions and compulsions that resulted from those undesirable thoughts.

Judy's mother expressed her need to understand the cause of her daughter's condition, thinking that if she understood the cause and more about this disorder, perhaps she could better support her daughter and help her reach the healing that she so desperately desired. As explained to both Judy and her mother, the exact cause of OCD is not completely known. Recent advances in technology have produced much better information about this and other psychiatric disorders; based on these studies, OCD seems to be linked to low levels of a chemical substance in the brain called serotonin. Serotonin is one of many natural chemicals stored in the nerves. Brain nerve cells need serotonin to send messages (electrical impulses) to other cells. Since serotonin helps to carry the message from one nerve cell to another, it is also called a neurotransmitter. The OCD patient has a diminished supply of serotonin; therefore this message sending function in the brain is somewhat impaired. Appropriate medications are used for the purpose of helping the patient's body to produce more of its own serotonin so that their chemical make-up can be rebalanced and thus function more efficiently.

In addition to brain chemistry and the decreased serotonin levels, available studies in the field also suggest other possible causal factors which include: (1) genetics, (2) childhood trauma, (3) stress, and (4) personality traits. Since OCD does tend to run in families with about 20-25% OCD patients having other family members who also experience this problem, it is felt there may be a genetic component. However, most clinicians treating it would suggest there is probably as much environmental influence in such situations as genetics since children will tend to imitate or follow the model set by parents or other adults in their world. If a child sees his or her parent extremely anxious about something, they tend to learn that same response to the same object. In a majority of patients suffering from OCD, symptoms began appearing in childhood. In reality, there is quite likely an interaction of both genetics and learning from the environment—thus the need for both medicine to alter the body chemistry and psychotherapy to help alter the previous learning and replace it with new thinking.

Some OCD patients reveal deep seated conflicts of early childhood trauma such as physical or sexual abuse, neglect, abandonment or similar catastrophe; in such cases, the OCD behaviors are more the symptom of the underlying, unresolved conflict. In about 25-30% cases of OCD, patients report a stressful event that was associated with the onset of the illness (i.e. death of loved one, accident, major life changes, abortion, trauma of sexual or physical abuse, loved one or friend contracting HIV, etc.). Many OCD patients have particular personality traits that tend to promote or give way to this illness—perfectionistic or rigid people.

Judy and her mother were desperate to try anything to help reduce the pain that she experienced daily; however, as with most patients they were concerned about taking medication and worried about possible side effects. Her mother also asked if this meant that Judy would need to be on this medication for the rest of her life. As explained to this very concerned mother, the medication used to re-balance the serotonin levels in the brain are not mind altering drugs and would not cause Judy to seem weird or bizarre. These medications were absolutely safe—quite likely safer than aspirin and Tylenol; such medications called Selective Serotonin Reuptake Inhibitors (SSRI's for short), were anti-depressants utilized to reduce depressive and anxiety related symptoms, panic attacks, OCD, discomfort associated with PMS and menopause, and even recently becoming useful in helping to reduce attention deficit disorder among other conditions. I further explained that SSRI's are not addictive and since they are not toxic, even an overdose would not cause death. The SSRI's essentially help one's body produce this chemical substance called serotonin which has for one reason or another become deficient in their body—thus helping their body chemistry to "rebalance" itself and promote better control of their cognitive functions (thinking) and emotional responses (feelings).

Asked if Judy would need to be on these medications for the rest of her life, her mother was reassured to learn that generally about 6—8 months of consistent dosing is long enough for the body to re-establish its own adequate serotonin production rate. I further explained that to avoid possible side effects, these medications are usually started at one-half the therapeutic dose and gradually increased until the normal dosage is achieved. Of course, both Judy and her mother seemed concerned about possible side effects. Again, they were reassured to learn that the side effects are minor and usually temporary, disappearing in a week or two after one's body has adjusted to the medication. Common side effects for SSRI medication may include: dry mouth, sleepiness, headache, tiredness, constipation, dizziness, insomnia, sexual libido problems, sweating, nausea, nervousness, insomnia, and either an increase or decrease in appetite. In discussing these possible side effects with Judy's mother, I could detect an immediate hesitancy in agreeing to have her daughter take one of these medicines. Again, I reassured this concerned mother that possible side effects are reported by FDA even if they occur in 1% of the patients participating in the pre-testing of the drug. For the most part, side effects are usually dosage related; and, since slowing down the introduction of the medication to one's body, side effects have become much less of a concern and most persons experience only minor or no side effects at all.

While working through these issues and seemingly accepting the explanations offered for each of these questions, Judy's mother then posed perhaps the biggest questions that most Christians either ask, or if not asked, remain quietly troubled by— "Why can't our faith in God and the many prayers that we pray for God to take this problem away from her solve it? Is God punishing her or even me for something that one of us has done? Is He trying to teach us something through having us go through such pain?"

Once again, I tried to reassure both Judy and her mother as I calmly responded, "I really cannot say that I have always understood the wisdom in God allowing His children to suffer with pain—especially pain that may be caused by others and not something that is the result of any of their own decisions or behavior. However, I guess it goes back to Adam and Eve and their decisions that brought sin into this world ... since that time, all mankind—both the believer and the nonbeliever—suffer from the presence of sin in the world." Referencing them to II Corinthians 12:9, I tried to reassure this precious mother and her daughter that God has promised to help us conquer any problem, no matter how enormous it may seem. I added, "Scripture tells us that His grace is sufficient for such challenges." I further shared that I didn't see anything in the nature of God to cause His children pain in order that they might learn something, become stronger, or more dependent upon Him—for God is omniscient, and with such wisdom, He must have a multitude of methods by which to teach His children such things without producing pain in their lives. I tried to explain that such things quite likely occur because of sin in the world; however, if we turn to Him and accept this grace that He has promised for such times, avoid becoming bitter over the unfairness that we feel, God can allow much learning to come from such adversities and we can become stronger as a result of them. I suggested to both Judy and her mother, "God can turn this terrible and painful thing into something positive ... I'm sure that God grieves with you as He sees the pain that both you and your daughter are experiencing!" While God does not exempt Christians from the torments of this life, He has promised to go with us through the valley! This thought can be reassuring to a patient struggling with self-doubt and wondering if God has deserted them during this time of crisis in their lives.

Judy's course of treatment was not without many discouraging times; however, she persevered and faithfully attempted to apply the learning she gained from each session. Initially, she was given a small yellow purse that closed with a side zipper. This purse became what we referred to as her "worry or thought" pouch; the pouch contained blank cards on which Judy was to write any thought or worry that became one of her obsessions. After writing it on the card, she was encouraged to put it outside of her mind since she had made a record of it for discussion at our next session. This technique of externalizing the thought or "releasing it from the mind" is facilitated if the patient makes a written record of the thought somewhere. Much of the time for the next few sessions was devoted toward processing these thoughts or worries with Judy. We developed a simple problem solving method by which Judy could either validate or invalidate the thought by asking herself some simple questions. The questions used in this process follow:

1. Is this thought logical or illogical? (Rational or irrational?)
2. Is this thought true or untrue? (Based on fact, or is it based on perception or feelings?)
3. Is this thought realistic or is it an exaggeration of something?

If Judy could conclude that the thought was not logical, true, or was an exaggeration, then she was instructed to dismiss it and not give any further time or energy to processing it in her mind, for to do so was to validate a thought that wasn't valid. To help her dismiss the thought from her mind rather than continue obsessing about it or worse yet, start the compulsive picking at her skin, Judy was instructed to place a large "**X**" through the written issue on the card with a wide marker and replace it in the worry pouch. She was further encouraged to immediately start a different activity that would help get her mind off the obsession. Such an activity serves as a diversion, and is hopefully incompatible with the obsessive thought or compulsive activity. Judy was asked to make a list of activities and hobbies that she had previously enjoyed; this became her menu of alternative activities that would help diminish the extremely painful obsessive thinking. The most successful activities were action oriented activities that hopefully required both hands to accomplish. Judy developed an interest in digital photography, painting, ceramics, and other arts & craft activities.

Whenever Judy started obsessing about something, she was advised to allow herself only ten minutes to work through the process involving the questions above, and then she would proceed to one of the alternate activities. This became a very helpful process in Judy gaining control over the obsessing behavior; the alternative activities served as a diversion and thus preventing the obsessive thinking from leading to the compulsive behavior. Judy was also coached to begin using "self-talk" daily; the self-talk statements she was asked to make included such things as:

(1) "I am now determined to conquer this problem; and, I know that with God's help I will do it!"
(2) "There are several options, other than picking my skin, to reduce my distress!"
(3) "I know that my obsessions are exaggerated and unrealistic!"
(4) "This thought is irrational … I am going to let it go!"
(5) "Now is not the time to think about it … I can think about it later."
(6) "I refuse to argue with an irrational thought!"
(7) "I don't have to figure out this question … the best thing to do is just drop it."
(8) "I already know from past experiences that these thoughts are irrational!"
(9) "It's ok that I just had that thought/image, and it doesn't mean anything. I don't have to give my attention to it; I can just turn it over to God!"

The self-talk statements was an attempt to begin helping Judy change her rather depressive, conditioned negative thinking; this procedure helped her learn that she could take control of her thoughts. As she became more optimistic and positive, the negative thinking began to disappear and the depression began to lift; Judy began to regain self confidence in conquering this problem. As she continued in treatment, her sullen and unsmiling countenance gave way to an occasional smile; and eventually, Judy reflected increased self assurance and seemed more at peace with herself.

As Judy's treatment continued over several months, the psychotherapy sessions helped her examine many of the causal factors that contributed to the development of her obsessions and subsequent compulsions that had taken over her life and robbed her of the contentment God desires for His children. It was learned that Judy and her mother attended a church that believed in holiness as a second work of grace. As a young child and desiring to make God the center of her life and follow the example that was set by her parents, she listened intently as her pastor frequently preached on this second work of grace. Judy shared that their pastor had frequently referred to holiness as "being perfect" and referenced Matthew 5:48 as his text for such a sermon. Judy explained that this verse says to "be perfect, therefore, as your heavenly Father is perfect!" In frustration she shared that she took this to heart as she really desired to be totally surrendered to God and gain this experience. Obviously, Judy had done what a multitude of Christians hearing the holiness message do when they hear the reference to "being perfect" or reaching "perfection"—they tend to forget that perfection is not possible so long as we are in this earthly body.

Her pastor needed to do a better job of explaining that God has commanded us to seek His image or to be more like Him; this perfection that He has commanded is an "ideal" and actually "perfection of heart" and not perfect performance. By surrendering our lives to Christ in total commitment to His will, we are seeking that the carnal nature of selfishness and self serving motives be replaced with whatever God desires our life to be. I shared with Judy that the "old timers" in my father's days use to call it "signing the blank check". By this they meant that when one asks God to sanctify him or herself, they are essentially telling God that they are making out the check for their entire life to Him and endorsing it— allowing Him to fill in the blank. This is what most holiness churches call "sanctification" or the second work of grace which follows salvation. While salvation is the act of asking God to forgive one of his sins and transgressions, sanctification is asking Him to take complete control of his or her life by totally committing or surrendering everything to Him. I tried to explain that Judy would never reach perfection, but if she surrendered her whole self to God, He would give her a "pure" heart. While she would probably still make human errors in judgment, her motives would remain pure and therefore she had what has become known as "holiness of heart" or a "perfect" heart.

Judy and her mother agreed that this explanation made sense and that by beginning to think in this direction, perhaps the previous learning could be replaced by this new knowledge. "But then what about that verse of scripture in I John 4:18 that says, ' ... there is no fear in love ... perfect love drives out fear' ... ?" asked Judy's mother. She continued by clarifying her concern, "If we are truly sanctified ... and I thought that we were ... why does Judy have such fear?"

Pausing for a moment to collect my thoughts, I then responded to her question with a gentle but direct response, "Do you know anyone on earth that is perfect?"

She answered, "No ... only Christ Himself was perfect here on earth!"

I continued, "Then we can't imply a literal meaning here, but more of a figurative one—meaning, if we surrender our whole life to Christ in this process of sanctification, then we need not worry for God will direct us to where He wants us to go ... essentially, we turn everything over to God and allow Him to completely rule our lives ... He controls our motives, desires, goals, aspirations, everything about us! The figurative meaning is that we don't have to fear, but that we can relax in the knowledge that God controls our life and everything about it!" I further explained that many people struggle with fear or anxiety from time to time. Satan doesn't waste his time trying to tempt the committed Christian with the typical sins—adultery, pornography, stealing, drugs, or alcohol. However, in his crafty, sneaky manner, if Satan can get the Christian to doubt his experience with God—cause increased doubt or fear that maybe what they felt they experienced was only an emotional response and didn't really have substance, then he might defeat that person and cause him or her to give up. Many Christians have given up on trying to serve God since they falsely came to a conclusion that they couldn't be perfect; some have even admitted to me, "I just can't live the perfect life ... I can't be perfect!" Unfortunately, these people have taken this perfection concept literally rather than as it was intended—a perfect heart.

I further explained to Judy and her mother that most theologians who endorse the concept of holiness as a second work of grace would describe it as a two step process: (1) the "crisis experience" or the conscious decision to totally surrender one's life to Christ and His service, and (2) progressive sanctification, which refers to the ongoing process of becoming more like Christ through spiritual maturation. Although we become more and more like Christ as we mature in following Him and our relationship deepens over time, we will not experience total perfection until we reach Heaven at which time we will have a completely new body without the "humanness" we experience here on earth. To help them understand this concept further, I referred this mother and her daughter to a scripture that talks about holiness as a condition of one's heart and a process, "Not that I have already obtained all this, or have already been made perfect, but I press on to take hold of that for which Christ Jesus took hold of me" (Phillipians 3:12). While God requires perfection as a goal, His grace accepts us as we are! No human being is perfect, nor will he or she ever accomplish perfection until reaching heaven. To insist on perfection in ourselves or others causes deep psychological problems!

Although the course of treatment for Judy involved several months, she did eventually finish her treatment successfully. The sores on her skin healed, leaving only minor scars that would remind her of this terrible time in her life as a young lady trying to find answers. The learning she gained from her sessions helped her accept a whole new philosophy of "BALANCE" for all areas of her life. She eventually was able to discontinue the SSRI medication that had helped to re-establish the chemical balance of her body; however, she vowed she would not hesitate to go back on this medication if her symptoms returned. Her social life as a young teenager seemed to blossom as she now had a significantly improved self-esteem and was not self-conscience about the sores on her arms and legs for they were gone. She became more involved in her church's youth program and took on some leadership roles for her youth pastor. After several months of prayerful consideration,

Judy's mother did divorce her husband as he had abandoned her and his family; there seemed to be no signs of reconciliatory efforts on his part. Judy's anger toward her father seemed to diminish over time; she expressed pity for him and concern for his soul rather than anger at what he did to her and her mother. She determined within her heart to avoid allowing her legitimate anger for what he did to them to turn into bitterness. Although moving on in her own life, she continued to pray that her father would find God and resolve the things in his life that led him to sin.

It is usually a happy occasion when that last official session is scheduled to bring closure to the treatment process. As I went to the waiting area to greet Judy and her mother, I couldn't help but remember that time when I first met Judy and the extreme pain that was exhibited by this young person. Today, several months later, I greeted a very different person! Judy had a smile on her face and her mother's countenance likewise did not reveal the deep concern and worry that had characterized that first meeting. Judy excitedly shared that this guy from her youth group had asked her to sit with him at the concert her church was sponsoring within the next couple of weeks. She knew this would be important to me as her therapist since I had predicted this might happen despite her earlier contention she would never date or get married. As we brought closure to the therapeutic relationship we had had over several months, the most rewarding thing that Judy shared was a beautiful testimony to knowing with confidence that she was saved and sanctified. With a glow on her face, she chuckled with a giggle that is characteristic only to teenage girls as she expressed, "Now that I know that holiness is not literally being perfect, but a perfect heart and motive, I can say with confidence, I am sanctified and in the center of God's will!"

Chapter 11

Sexual Identity Problems—
Is There A Cause?
What's the Cure?

Perhaps one of the most challenging issues the church—a mission station for lost souls—must face in today's culture is the issue of homosexuality. For many years, the church was able to ignore it as if it was one of those secular elements so foreign to the church that it could be safely ignored and no one would seem to notice. But unfortunately, those churches that were inspired to accept God's command to fulfill the Great Commission could no longer ignore this issue. Dr. Norman Wilson, a well known leader in the Wesleyan Church, has said that whatever condition one finds within society, that same condition will also be represented in the church fulfilling its purpose of evangelizing the lost. In recent years, the questions regarding this issue have not merely rested with whether such an individual should be welcomed at the church, the saint's comfort level, or acceptance of the fact that all persons have souls regardless of their sinful behavior or lifestyle. Certainly the church should welcome every type of person— Christ came to save whosoever would believe on Him! The church is in many ways the facility—the mission station— that helps to accomplish the Great Commission. As an old witticism conveys, "the church is a hospital for the sinner ... not a rest home for the saint."

In current times, the issues causing much debate in religious organizations and denominations goes much further than mere welcoming the person struggling with homosexuality into attendance at our churches, it now involves requests for full acceptance into church membership, opportunities to serve in leadership to others, being appointed as deacons or elders, and even ordination into the ministry or priesthood. There is much debate of this subject and the relevant issues; it is causing much division and is even splitting major denominations. While we believe the Bible teaches that all homosexual conduct is wrong, contrary to God's Word, and we must uphold this standard of holiness, we must also reflect God's love and redemptive power to change whosoever would choose to follow Him. The Bible clearly delineates that heterosexuality is God's creative intent for humanity and that any expression of homosexuality is sin. Genesis 1:26—31 documents God's creation of " ... male and female ... God blessed them and said ... Be fruitful and increase in number ... fill the earth ... " Matthew 19:1-6 elaborates, " ... the Creator made them male and female, and said, for this reason a man will leave his father and mother and be united to his wife, and the two will become one flesh."

Perhaps by expanding our understanding of homosexuality, the contributing causal factors, the appropriate treatment and recovery process, the church will be better capable of ministering to these people who deserve God's love like everyone else in society. Heterosexuality is defined by most authorities to mean the sexual attraction, expression of affection, and the union between two persons of the opposite sex—male and female. Homosexuality is the sexual attraction, and sexual or affectional preference for members of the same sex—male with another male or female with another female. While female homosexuals are frequently referred to as "lesbians", male homosexuals are usually referred to as "gays" although at times both sexes might be called "gays". The term "gay" is one of the few terms applied to homosexuals that have been adopted by them as a sign of pride. There are also several negative terms used to refer to people practicing or endorsing the homosexual lifestyle; these usually have a derogatory or critical tone implied. A lesbian who takes a stereotyped masculine role in the relationship is referred to as "dyke", while the gay man who assumes the stereotyped feminine role is frequently referred to as "fairy." "Straight" is the term used by heterosexuals, lesbians, and gay men to refer to people who believe in and practice heterosexuality. "In the closet" refers to lesbians or gay men who feel unable to tell others that they are gay; gays may not be open with their sexual preference to avoid discrimination or rejection on their jobs or from friends and family. "Coming out of the closet" is a metaphor for telling people about one's lesbian or gay identity; "coming out" was a phrase adopted by gay people to describe the process of becoming aware of and expressing one's identity. Perhaps a very negative reference for the gay population is the word "faggot" which is from a Latin word meaning "a bundle of sticks"; this term was applied to gays during the Inquisition when they were burned along with "witches" during that period in history.

Although slightly different than homosexuality, there are some related practices that will probably also be represented in the attendance of a church focused on fulfilling the Great Commission. These persons represent a digression from the heterosexual lifestyle. Several years ago, in an attempt to compromise on the strict differences between homosexuality and heterosexuality, society started promoting the acceptance of and even teaching that "androgynous" traits could help resolve the conflicts between these two lifestyles. Androgynous comes from the Greek words "andre" meaning man and "gyne" meaning woman, and essentially suggests that a person with androgynous traits possess both masculine and feminine traits. Many researchers and much of the secular mental health movement suggest this as the mental health ideal. "Bi-sexuals" are those people who claim to have sexual and emotional interests toward both sexes; such persons practice both homosexual and heterosexual sexuality and frequently having sexual partners of both sexes. Very different than the homosexual, the "transsexual" is the person who feels he or she really belongs to the opposite sex; this person feels "trapped" in a physical body of one sex, but having the emotional make-up and interests of the opposite sex. To resolve this inner conflict, this person undergoes multiple surgeries and hormonal treatments to be changed into the opposite sex. A "transvestite" is a man or a woman who gets erotic pleasure from dressing in opposite sex clothing; transvestites are thought to have homosexual urges but rather than act these out sexually, they engage their fantasy through dramatizing the opposite sex by wearing that gender's clothing.

It is the position of this author and churches within the holiness denominations that heterosexuality is God's creative intent for all mankind and that any expression of homosexuality is outside of God's will. Scripture clearly supports this position! Paul describes homosexuality as a wicked perversion of God's gift , " ... God gave them over to shameful lusts ... women exchanged natural relations for unnatural ones ... men also abandoned natural relations with women and were inflamed with lust for one another ... men committed indecent acts with other men ... "(Romans 1:26-7). Homosexual tendencies are one of the many disorders that beset our humanity. Choosing to act out or resolve these tendencies through the expression of homosexual behavior (" ... wicked will not inherit the kingdom of God ... neither the sexually immoral ... adulterers ... male prostitutes nor homosexual offenders ... " I Corinthians 6:9-11), or taking on a homosexual identity (" ... what counts is a new creation" Galations 6:15), or involvement in the homosexual lifestyle (" ... put off your old self ... corrupted by deceitful desires ... put on the new self, created to be like God in true righteousness and holiness" Ephesians 4:17-24) is sin; it is certainly destructive and distorts God's intent for the individual. It becomes the church's responsibility to represent the healing that Christ offers through redemption whereby sin's power over the individual is broken and he or she can become a new creation in Christ Jesus. As II Corinthians 5:17 says, " ... if anyone is in Christ, he is a new creation; the old has gone, the new has come!" This thought is further elaborated by Romans 12:2 which reads, "do not conform any longer to the pattern of this world, but be transformed by the renewing of your mind ... then you will be able to test and approve what God's will is."

Following conversion, sin's power is broken and the individual experiences a freedom to know and experience true identity through Christ and His church. This freedom allows for healing that involves a process of growing into heterosexuality and resolution of the distortions in thinking that had been accepted as truth and normal. For several years, many Christians and some churches have responded to homosexual men and women with ignorance and fear—thus failing to fulfill the Great Commission. It is high time the church and those of us, who make up the church, take a more appropriate role in ministering to those who have fallen into this particular sin. By showing acceptance of the person and helping the homosexual understand forgiveness and the possibility of transformation to a new life, we are not endorsing or accepting the sin. We are merely being Christlike; Christ accepts and loves the sinner while never condoning the sinful nature.

Jerry was a well dressed, handsome young man in his early twenties; he had been referred for treatment by his pastor after he confessed that he was struggling with his sexual identity. Although his pastor had attempted to counsel with him a couple of times from a pastoral counseling perspective and helping him understand the scriptural view of the problem, Jerry continued to struggle with what he referred to as "the war within my mind" over his sincere desire to serve God and the strong urges and confusion he experienced regarding his sexuality. Sitting alone in my waiting room on the day of his first appointment, Jerry appeared quite distressed. My secretary had shared with me that he had completed the initial paper work for registering him as a new patient and authorizing treatment, but had not written anything under the section of the form that asks for presenting problems. I reassured her that I had already spoken to his pastor who had referred him to me and that she wouldn't need to ask him to complete that section on the form. Over the years of working with patients, I have learned that while some patients are willing to honestly share their concerns with me, it is too difficult for them to put those issues down on paper—thus completing all sections of the information form except this one that asks for a summary of the concerns bringing them to treatment. After greeting Jerry in the waiting room, I invited him to my office. As we passed by the coffee, I asked him if he would like a cup of coffee and he agreed. With a cup of coffee in both our hands, we entered my office and closed the door for privacy. Although somewhat uncomfortable and appearing nervous, Jerry seemed more relaxed since the cup of coffee gave him something to do with his hands.

I began our discussion with an opening remark, "Your pastor called and talked with me one day last week to let me know you would be calling to set up an appointment; however, he didn't give me many details of the reason for seeking treatment ... could you summarize for me the concerns that prompted you to see me?"

Jerry cleared his throat nervously, and then responded. "I am struggling with my sexuality ... I have a lot of confusion in that area ... I know what the Bible says about homosexuality and I really want to be a Christian, but I seem to struggle with an interest in and sexual urges for other men rather than women." Recognizing this was extremely hard for him to articulate to me—a stranger whom he had only met a few moments before, I reassured him that this problem is experienced by many young people his age and that his pastor did the right thing by asking him to see me. As typical for any such problem, I proceeded with gathering historical data that would help me better define when and how this problem developed. Jerry seemed to relax after sharing the reason he had sought treatment; his responses to the additional questions I asked were given without any hesitation. He was actually a good historian and I could tell he had given considerable thought to this issue; he had probably had plenty of sleepless nights as he struggled with the turmoil between his head knowledge of the Scriptural views on homosexuality and the physiological urges he was experiencing as a young man in his early twenties.

Jerry shared that he was one of two children born to his parents; he had an older brother who was now 28, married, and had two children. He described his relationship with his brother to be "okay ... although I feel that if I was married and had a child, we might have more in common and would perhaps be closer." When asked about his relationship with his parents, he replied, "Well, I am closer to my mother than my father; it seems like I was closer to my mother and my older brother was closer to my father ... my mother seems to understand me more." I asked if he had any ideas why he was more attached to his mother while his brother had a similar attachment to his father. Jerry responded, "I think that my dad found it easier to relate to my brother who was interested in sports and hunting which were interests my father also had ... I never really took to sports, instead I focused more of my time on music rather than playing sports ... I don't think my dad could appreciate my music like he did my brother's sports." As is often the case in such family situations, Jerry's mother sensed her husband's difficulty and reluctance to affirm their son's interest in music and tried to make up for her husband's deficit in their son's life. Feeling more affirmation from his mother, Jerry naturally began spending more time with her; he began seeking her approval rather than his father's.

Although Jerry's mother recognized he really needed his father's attention as well as hers, she was reluctant to confront her husband's passive rejection of him and found herself enjoying this attachment as it was providing fulfillment for her. While she had hoped for at least one daughter to mother, God had given them two sons rather than a daughter. Since Jerry spent an inordinate amount of time with his mother, he began emulating some of her traits and learned to respond to things in more of an emotional manner than his brother who spent equivalent amounts of time with his father. Obviously, Jerry's brother learned from his father's role model; he began to emulate his father's masculine reactions to things and his response to situations appeared less emotional.

Within the very first session, Jerry was beginning to disclose some typical family dynamics observed in the homes of individuals that struggle with homosexuality—a confusion in the identification with the liked sex parent. Although most Christians reject Sigmund Freud and his psychoanalytical theory as a worldly, secular approach that is inconsistent with scripture, a closer look at his hypotheses on which his theory is based reveals some concepts that might hold relevance in understanding one of the many causal factors in homosexuality. Much of Freud's theory seems weird and highly sexualized; his writings seem to portray that every activity of mankind is linked somehow to his sexuality and sexual urges. However, we must not forget that what Freud was documenting for science was a recording of what his patients were sharing with him in psychoanalysis. Freud began his career in the late 1800's as a physician and neurologist. He became interested in psychological issues as a result of his experiences with patients who were suffering from paralysis of the legs or arms that seemed to lack any physiological cause—hysteria. His final theories represent a lifelong career of observing many kinds of neurotic patients and attempting to analyze the unconscious aspects of his own personality. When one reviews Freud's life and his personal beliefs, they are usually surprised to learn that he believed personally that any kind of sexual relationships with a purpose other than producing children was morally wrong. His hypothesis and subsequent theory was developed on his work with his patients who had unresolved conflicts regarding sexuality. Freud is considered the "father of psychology" and is credited with formulation of the Psychoanalytical Theory. A part of this theory is the Psychosexual Stages of Child Development. According to Freud, the child's normal development progresses through the following stages:

1. **Oral Stage (birth to 18 months):** gratification comes from mouth, sucking, infant very narcissistic
2. **Anal (18 months to 4 years):** child experiences excretion and toilet training, retention/elimination skills mastered
3. **Phallic (5 years to 7 years):** child is preoccupied with genitals, boys experience the Oedipus Complex and girls experience the Electra complex as identification task is accomplished
4. **Latency (7 years to puberty):** erotic desires repressed for attachment to like-sexed parent
5. **Genital (12 years to adulthood):** group activities, marriage, establishment of a home, development of vocation, career, job, etc.

In primarily the Phallic Stage but continuing into the Latency Stage for some children, Freud's theory suggests that both girls and boys accomplish a developmental task called "identification" which ultimately leads to the child formulating an identity to the like sexed parent. Little boys go through what he called the "Oedipus Complex." According to Freud's theory, at about age five the little boy begins to have sexual cravings or desires for his mother. While he sees that he cannot compete with his father for the mother's affection, he reasons and thus decides to become like his father in hopes of gaining the same attention he sees that she shows toward his father. The little boy begins to emulate or model after his father's traits, thus beginning the process of identification with the same sexed parent. The little girl, likewise goes through what Freud referenced as the "Electra Complex." At about age five, the little girl begins to have sexual cravings or desires for her father. While she sees that she cannot compete with her mother who has gained the father's full affection, she decides to become like her mother. The little girl begins to emulate or model after her mother's traits and mannerisms, thus the process of identification with the same sexed parent occurs. It is her hope that if she becomes like her mother, she will gain the approval and hopefully the affection of her father.

Now quite frankly, having worked with children for the past twenty-five years, I have never encountered a five year old child who truly desired his mother or father sexually. Most five year olds are not aware of sexuality and certainly do not have sexual urges for their parent. But Freud's theorem on the importance of identifying with the same sexed parent seems to have validity. A vast majority of the patients struggling with homosexual problems that I have seen in therapy over the last several years have disclosed family histories that would suggest many of their problems in thinking, emotional responsiveness, interests, and behavior can be traced back to not having accomplished this identification task appropriately. Instead of taking on the attributes of the like sexed parent, focus on the opposite sexed parent takes place and through perhaps a closer more meaningful relationship with that parent, emulation of his or her traits results.

In the case of Jerry, he had not been encouraged to identify with his father, but instead permitted to identify and begin taking on like mannerisms and attributes of his mother—thus becoming more "feminine" in nature. This can happen in single parent families where the like sexed parent is absent, thus leaving the child only one parent to model if other substitute role models are not available. It can also occur in abusive homes where the like sexed parent is abusive and the child is drawn to the opposite sexed parent for protection. Instead of emulating the "abusive" parent, the child is encouraged to model after the opposite sexed parent. Without opportunity to learn appropriate behaviors, emotional responses, mannerisms, interests, and attitudes through modeling after the like sexed parent, the child usually models after the other parent and thus has severe deficits in his psychosexual development. As the child matures, the differences he or she feels from peers becomes greater and with this results increased confusion. It is easy for the teenager or adult to feel they were in fact born with this inclination since they remember the confusion dating back to a very early age. When asked how long he had experienced these feelings, Jerry said, "From as early as I can remember, I have had confusion over this issue ... I think I must have really been born with these traits and the attraction to males rather than the opposite sex."

Jerry shared that as he got older and became more aware of the differences he felt in comparison to peers, he began to accept these traits as his own—thus becoming a significant part of his identity or self-image. During teenage years, he took much verbal abuse from classmates. As he felt unaccepted by the majority of his peer group both at school and church, he became more of a loner. As his discomfort increased, he attended fewer social events and became more inhibited socially. Although he spent much time in developing his musical abilities in both voice and keyboard, the lack of approval or affirmation from his father continued to reinforce the fragile self-esteem Jerry had managed to develop on his own. Jerry reported that he could easily see that his father was greatly pleased with his brother's increasing abilities in both football and soccer; but, that he seldom expressed any appreciation for Jerry's long hours of practice or musical performances at school or church. In an effort to defend his father, Jerry said, "I really just don't think my father knew how to relate to me since I am not like him or have the same interests ... I do think that he loved me ... at least I hope he did ... does ... I guess he does love me, after all, I'm his son."

In future sessions, Jerry disclosed that as he got into later teen years, he began exploring pornography. First looking at heterosexual literature and videos, he then progressed to bi-sexual material which rapidly progressed into materials designed for gays. The more he read about homosexuality, the more rationale he found for the way he felt. The literature conveyed that the confusion most gays feel is their denial of their gayness and that "coming out" would help him reach happiness and end the turmoil he experienced. While wishing he could experience more peace, Jerry said he never had enough courage to declare his "gayness" as he knew that such disclosure would severely hurt his parents and damage their reputation within their church. In describing his church, Jerry said, "My church was one that didn't have any tolerance for any form of sin and I'm sure they would not hesitate to declare me a sinner if I even hinted that I was questioning my sexuality ... it was okay if I was a little weird or different, but to share questions regarding sexual orientation would surely bring on my death sentence ... they would probably want to excommunicate me from the church!"

This fear had kept Jerry's secret a secret; it also probably prevented him from sharing the problem with those who could have directed him to appropriate treatment in the earlier stages of the problem. Instead, the problem worsened; the once uncomfortable feelings of guilt became less and by at least pretending that he could believe what the gay literature conveyed that he must have been born this way—a genetic predisposition as they describe—excused him for not attempting to change his thinking. If he was born this way, Jerry rationalized that he might as well accept his gayness; he was beginning to feel that it could not be changed! The more he continued in this vein of thinking, the more depressed he got; Jerry was rapidly coming to the conclusion that he could not alter this pattern of thinking and behavior, he was losing hope!

Jerry finished high school and went off to college to begin preparation for a career in teaching music. While the university environment is usually a rather rich atmosphere for stimulating young people to question everything—even the value system they have come to believe from their upbringing, Jerry found college life to only add more conflict to his turmoil. Being a music major, he was required to spend several hours in practice rooms in the music studio. One night while finishing his practice time and beginning to leave his assigned practice room, he was surprised to be interrupted by a classmate who said he wanted to be Jerry's friend. This guy told Jerry that since he was new at the university, he might need an upperclassman to help show him around. As the conversation continued, this new self-appointed friend proceeded to share with Jerry that he was gay and could tell that Jerry was gay as well. He said he had been watching him for several days and had even made a few invitational gestures but Jerry had apparently not noticed them. This guy told Jerry that he currently had a lover, but he desired to have sex with Jerry. Jerry was both frightened and overwhelmed; but then he remembered that he had come to believe that his orientation was genetic and since he couldn't alter it, maybe the literature he had read about just "coming out" and accepting his gayness would bring an end to his confusion and pain. Although frightened about this encounter, Jerry found himself compromising and within a few minutes found himself in this guy's apartment which culminated in Jerry performing oral sex with this homosexual man.

Jerry said, "I thought I was confused before ... now I was really confused!" Jerry left to return to his dorm for a sleepless night. Jerry laid awake reviewing all the things he had learned about sexuality; he reviewed what he had learned from Sunday school and discussions regarding this issue in his youth group. But no matter how hard he thought, he could not bring resolution to the gulf between what he knew in his head that this behavior was sinfully wrong and how he felt emotionally so drawn to this form of sexual acting out. The next day, Jerry looked for this guy who said he had wanted to become Jerry's friend. He finally found him, but to Jerry's surprise, the guy ignored Jerry. When finally Jerry got his attention and asked him about showing him around, the guy told him to find some other "experienced guy" to "show him the ropes."

Jerry later learned that this guy had a regular live-in gay lover and that this one night encounter with Jerry was typical for him. He also learned that many gays consider "having sex" with another gay is okay and not unfaithful to one's lover so long as it is just for physical release and there isn't any relationship or emotional intimacy tied into the act.

Jerry confessed in a later session that there had been three or four other such encounters; he reported that one had been with one of his instructors—a doctoral student who was hired to be an instructor for underclassmen. To Jerry's surprise, each of these subsequent encounters likewise wasted no time with development of a relationship prior to suggesting sexual contact. Reluctantly, Jerry disclosed that the oral sex had progressed to anal sex and this frightened him so much that he decided to discuss his confusion with someone. He remembered in his freshman orientation activities being told that as a student, he could see a counselor through student services. Thinking this would help guard against his parents discovering his recent activities, he arranged to see a counselor. Although feeling better to have talked with someone about his dilemma, Jerry said this counselor took a very secular view on the issue; rather than helping him clarify his confusion, he told Jerry that he probably was gay and that he shouldn't feel guilty about his recent sexual encounters as this just symbolized his trying to figure out what he wanted. Jerry said it was clear to him that this counselor knew nothing about what the Bible said about homosexuality as he never once even mentioned or questioned the issue of morality.

After several more sleepless nights and continued turmoil resulting in a rather crisis oriented depression, Jerry decided to call his mother and talk with her at least in general terms about his crisis. Without telling her about the specific issue, Jerry told her he was struggling in college and wanted to come home. That next morning, Jerry withdrew from college, packed his belongings into his car, and made the long drive of five hours home. After arriving home, he told his mother that he wanted to talk with their pastor. She told him that while he had been gone for those few months, their old pastor had left to take a different church and a new one had been selected. She described him as a younger man in comparison to the first and assured Jerry that he would like him. Jerry did meet with his new pastor who had a compassionate heart for the pain that Jerry bore; without judgment or condemnation on Jerry, he listened and after Jerry was exhausted from talking, he led Jerry to recommit his heart to Christ. Several days later, Jerry came to my office to seek clinical treatment of his problem. He had been forgiven of the sin; now he needed to work through the process of treatment.

Jerry's treatment consisted of several steps; while his forgiveness and transformation to a new life was instantaneous and took place the instant he demonstrated genuine remorse for his sins and asked God to forgive him, the process of changing his thinking and those personality attributes that had become a part of the lifestyle he was leaving would change slowly over the course of months or even years. As explained to Jerry in one of his sessions, homosexuality is a complex problem and while quite possible to find a way out, it is not an easy process. Although the gay movements would not like to admit it, there are thousands who have left homosexuality behind and have become a "new creation in Christ." Much of the literature produced from Christian organizations focused on helping people leave this lifestyle such as Love In Action, Metanoia Ministries, Transformation Ministries, and Exodus International suggest that deliverance comes from a person, rather than a method. Of course that person is Jesus Christ and for this reason the person seeking deliverance must get to know God better than anyone else in his or her life. Christ must become more important than friends, family, spouse, if the person is married, and even life itself.

Starting with his salvation as the foundation, Jerry was encouraged to nurture daily his walk with Christ. The Holy Spirit had brought conviction on Jerry's life and after several promptings, Jerry finally responded by surrendering his heart to Christ. Jerry had completed **the first step of recovery—conviction of his sins and agreement that homosexual activities are sin.** Jerry was encouraged to make a Bible study out of the verses of scripture shared earlier which would help to serve as his argument against the former lifestyle and help him resist the many temptations that would occur along the path to full recovery. He had likewise already accomplished the **second step—repentance and total surrender to God.** Remembering his upbringing, Jerry could not get away from the training he had experienced from both his parents and Sunday school teachers. He remembered Romans 10:9 which provided a way out, "If you confess with your mouth Jesus as Lord, and believe in your heart that God raised Him from the dead, you shall be saved." While Jerry desired peace from the turmoil he experienced, he had to come to a place of repentance; additionally, he had to be willing to totally surrender his life to God. This total surrender process is what holiness churches refer to as sanctification, or the second work of grace. Totally surrendering one's life to God is giving Him complete control. Committed to changing his life style, Jerry sought sanctification and made that surrender at an altar service two weeks after he had repented in the pastor's office.

Much like alcoholism, homosexuality or any form of sexual addictive behavior will not be resolved by oneself; this is why the well known treatment approach for alcoholism, Alcoholics Anonymous insists that the alcoholic learn to rely on "a higher power" to help him or her remain sober. Of course for the Christian, this higher power is God. No person will come out of homosexuality without total dependence upon God—therefore, this total surrender, or perhaps receiving the second work of grace through sanctification is an absolute pre-requisite in recovery! It's been said that God will take 99 of the 100 steps toward the believer, but the final step of consecration and total submission is a step that the individual must make. When that step is taken, holiness of heart can become a reality!

The **third step of recovery could be referred to as continued submission—the commitment made to Christ must be life long.** As soon as the ex-homosexual person feels he is far enough away from that lifestyle that he can manage on his or her own, Satan will provide rather dramatic temptations that can and often causes set-backs. The temptation may take the form of seeing an old acquaintance or hearing from a past companion, receiving an unsolicited e-mail from someone of the homosexual orientation to chat on the internet, or perhaps a small compromise to just peek at a pornographic website to "test" his or her recovery. Romans 12:2 and Ephesians 4:22-3 must become key verses of scripture for the recovering homosexual, he or she must remind themselves daily that they have been "transformed by the renewing of (their) mind ... " and that they have put off the old self which "was corrupted by its deceitful desires ... put on the new self, created to be like God in true righteousness and holiness." Many Christian therapists would refer to this process as "inner-healing."

In an attempt to prepare him for the attacks of Satan, I cautioned Jerry early on in his treatment that he would be tempted to return to the old ways. I encouraged him to build up several boundaries around him that would prevent him from slippage. He must sever any and all former relationships, even if merely casual ones, with anyone associated with the gay life. As a **fourth step in recovery—finding a new network or friends and support system,** Jerry was encouraged to develop new friends within the church or religious organizations on campus that would help provide fellowship within a safety network and accountability. He was encouraged to discuss with his pastor the possibility of connecting with a man in his church who could serve as an accountability partner and would mentor him over the coming months as he progressed through treatment. Being a small church with still having remnants of the traditional thinking that would reject or pose harsh judgment on Jerry, his pastor wisely decided to provide that role himself. The pastor felt the size of his congregation and work load made such involvement possible. Once a week, Jerry and his new pastor met for lunch or breakfast and a time of prayer and sharing. Jerry transferred his college credits to the local community college to continue pursuing his college education. Within time, he joined a couple of Christian organizations on campus—Youth For Christ and a small Bible study consisting of students from various programs. He slowly gained new friends and began feeling a sense of "belongingness."

The **fifth step of recovery for Jerry was altering behavioral patterns—changing the mannerisms and personality features that are associated with gays.** The new connection Jerry had with his pastor who was mentoring him was significant in helping provide a model for appropriate masculine features. Jerry desired to emulate his pastor—a young man whom Jerry had come to deeply respect. Jerry admired his pastor's concern for him and the church he pastored. He could see that this pastor loved his wife and children and spent good quality time with them. Even though this pastor was musically talented which provided a means of connecting with Jerry due to these common interests, Jerry observed the appropriate masculine role model that he needed to alter his own behaviors that seemed to resemble more feminine traits. While not criticizing Jerry, the pastor gradually and lovingly provided constructive feedback to Jerry as they worked together on changing the manner in which he carried himself, verbally responded to others, his selection of clothing, hair style, and other personal characteristics. Gradually, Jerry was changing the behaviors that others used to make judgments about him; he was learning to relate and act more like the norm—fitting into the new life he had chosen to live.

As Jerry progressed in treatment and became more confident with his new life style, I decided to request that Jerry consider inviting his parents to attend one of his sessions where he could share with them the struggles that he had experienced and help them understand the recent changes in his behaviors and mannerisms. Although Jerry had been a very cooperative patient and always took his assignments and suggestions seriously, he reacted with some hesitation at this request. I explained that he could share whatever he wanted to share and that all the details about his homosexual encounters at college wouldn't necessarily need to be shared. Still reluctant, I asked him to pray about it and assured him that we could prepare for such a meeting in the session that preceded it. At the next session, Jerry shared that he had prayed about it and had also discussed it with his pastor; he had concluded that it was a good idea and so the session was scheduled. The remaining time that day was spent strategizing and trying to predict his parent's questions, response, and predictable reactions. I assured Jerry that I would guide the session and would certainly intervene if I thought things were going astray or cause further hurt for the family.

The family session took place that following week. Everyone including myself seemed somewhat nervous about the agenda of this meeting. After small talk and expressing my appreciation for their son whom I had come to really enjoy working with over the previous months, I set the tone of the meeting by saying, "I'm sure you have seen some very positive changes in Jerry over the last several weeks."

They agreed and Jerry's father commented, "Jerry seems so much more focused and happy since he came home and started attending the local college rather than that big university."

I continued, "Well, I thought Jerry would like to share a few things with you so that you might better understand him and the changes he is making. Let's begin by asking God to be a part of this session."

After a brief prayer asking God to direct our session, I asked Jerry to share the things he felt his parents should know. Somewhat nervous as he began, Jerry verbalized, "Well, mom and dad, first of all I want you to know that you are very good parents and what I'm going to share with you has nothing to do with any failure on your part ... you taught me right and that's the reason I'm back in the church and serving God today! But as I was growing up, I developed some feelings that sort of led me astray and I started thinking that I was homosexual ... I thought for a while it couldn't be helped ... I almost began believing what the homosexual community has promoted for years that this sexual preference is genetic, you are born with it and it cannot be changed. Going to the university with an even more liberal group of kids and professors didn't help me at all; in fact, it seemed to further validate it at first. However, after accepting this sinful thinking as normal for awhile, God got a hold of my heart and I remembered my upbringing and what you and my Sunday School teachers taught me ... and I decided to come back home—both literally to our family and to the family of God."

By this time, both Jerry's parents were tearing up. "Was it anything that I did, son?" asked Jerry's father.

Jerry quickly responded, "Dad, I'm not blaming you or mom or anyone else for that matter. I'm taking full responsibility for the choices I made."

Jerry's mother then added, "I know I should have encouraged your father to have a closer relationship with you as he did your brother; I guess I'm partially to blame."

Again, Jerry responded swiftly, "Mom, you didn't do anything wrong; you were merely trying to comfort me and help me feel better about myself." At this point, I interjected and gave some clinical analysis to help Jerry's parents understand that perhaps the family dynamics contributed toward the development of his sexual confusion, but that they didn't do this purposefully and they should not blame themselves for this error.

As the session progressed, Jerry affirmed his parents several times for his upbringing and gave them credit for their Godly teaching for he felt strongly that had he not had this kind of childhood, he never would have found his way out of the homosexual lifestyle that he had begun. He didn't share the details of his sexual encounters and that he had undergone a complete physical exam to test for HIV and all other sexually transmitted diseases at my recommendation. They expressed how proud they were of him and his recent increased involvement at church since he had been asked to join the music ministry team and had also shared some musical specials for the congregation with the pastor. Both parents hugged their son with a very warm and affirming exchange at the conclusion of our session. Jerry's father concluded the session with these words, "Son, you could not have made me more proud ... I thank God for you and the multiple talents he has given you ... I only wish that I could have more of what God blessed you with ... but most of all, I am so thankful that you have chosen to use them for the Kingdom of God ... nothing could make your mother and I more pleased with you!"

Perhaps the most challenging change for Jerry was my insistence that he begin dating girls. While not openly resisting this suggestion, he was fearfully hesitant as he argued, "I just don't have any feelings for women ... I wouldn't know what to say ... I would look and feel so dumb ... I'm sure no one would ever go out with me a second time." With continual prodding, Jerry finally began going out with groups of young people and eventually got enough courage to ask a girl to a function sponsored by the Youth

For Christ Fellowship of which he belonged at the local college where he attended. The entire session which followed that "date" was devoted to processing that event and the extremely emotional responses Jerry felt. Through discussion, he was finally able to accept that his discomfort was not a sign of not having a hetero-sexual interest, but mostly anxiety from lack of practice. I encouraged him to continue having such dates, assuring him that he would become less anxious and build some confidence in this—perhaps one of the final challenges he faced in this fifth step of recovery in changing his behavioral patterns. Although some would fail at this step, Jerry persevered and eventually conquered this final step.

At the time of terminating his treatment with me, Jerry had found a young lady whom he had dated consistently for six months. As the relationship got more serious and it appeared as if the two would consider marriage, Jerry asked my advice concerning sharing with her his clouded past life. I advised him that as I understood marriage, there cannot be any secrets between a husband and his wife. Upon my advice, Jerry disclosed his past to this young lady. Somewhat anxious as he prepared to share this information with the woman he hoped would soon be his wife, he expressed that this would be the true test of their love for each other. A committed Christian that had grown immensely over the previous months as he deepened his relationship with Christ, Jerry shared that this matter was in God's hands and if He desired that they marry He would work out the details of this potential problem.

"After all, it is only right that the person I marry should know me transparently; it was only when I became transparent with God and those who loved me that I conquered the battle that raged within me" Jerry added. I assured him of my prayers, but somehow was confident that God would work a miracle and further healing would come to Jerry as a result of him being completely honest with his fiancée. Although worrying about the possible ramifications, Jerry did what he felt was God's leading and disclosed his past life to this young woman. To his surprise, she expressed how appreciative she was of his total honesty with her. Apparently, she told Jerry if he could be that transparent with her about the poor decision making he had done in his past, she was sure he was the one she wished to marry. Of course, she and those of us who knew Jerry, knew that his life was a living testimony of a life that had been transformed —he had chosen to allow God to transform him and decided to never look back!

Chapter 12

Internet Pornography— Newest Threat To The Church & Family

Research studies on the pornographic industry report it has grown to a $13-14 billion a year industry which is larger than the combined revenues reported by Coca-Cola and McDonnell Douglas Corporations. (1) In a recent article published in New Man Magazine, Eric Tiansay (2) reports that 300 million X-rated videos were distributed in 1990; since then, there has been a 75% rise in sales and rentals of adult videos, bringing current data to 525 million X-rated videos distributed annually. Officials of Promise Keepers report that 50% of the men attending these events around the country admit that they have engaged in some form of pornography within the week preceding the conference; a recent survey of this same group revealed that 2/3 had been or were currently involved with pornography. (3)

A recent article published in Christian Counseling Today further describes this epidemic in our society, "billions of dollars are made off of lust, sexual perversion, and sexual addiction … pornography has a pervasive presence in America and there seems to be no stopping it." (4) In addition to these figures, there are a multitude of R rated movies—considered to be soft porn, that are rented each year. Recent studies conducted by the Justice Department report that there are 280,000 X-rated web sites; this is an increase from 28,000 reported only 3 years ago. (5) Over a three year period of time there has been greater than 1000% growth. Focus on the Family report that 51% of pastors say that Internet pornography is a possible temptation to them; a Christianity Today Leadership survey revealed that more than 1/3 or 37% of pastors report it to be a current struggle in their spiritual life. (6) While statistics reported by Focus on the Family indicate that in the year 2000, 1 in 5 adults (or 20%, which is nearly 40 million people) have visited a sexually oriented web site, other data reveals that 4 out of 10 or 40% of pastors report they have personally visited a pornographic web site. (7)

Most experts report that of the total number of websites on the internet, more than half—reaching 60% in recent years, are pornographic. By the year 2005, it is projected that Americans will spend over $300,000,000 a year on Internet, fee-based websites. (8) Christians have for years felt threatened by what Hollywood produces in films, but did you know that there are 11,000 pornographic films produced each year—20 times more than what Hollywood produces for the movie film industry? (9) Some clinicians in the mental health fields who offer treatment for addictions estimate conservatively that as much as 6-10 percent of the adult population is sexually addicted. (10) To foolishly discount this threat and say that it is only a problem for the world and doesn't challenge the church or Christian world would be totally irrational! We live in a very sexually oriented society; our culture promotes sexually explicit material across almost every aspect of our lives. "Sex appeal" is used by the advertising industry to market everything from perfume to automobiles. The vast majority of advertisements seen in magazines, on television, or even on billboards along the highways we drive each day will contain some image that is designed to attract the on-looker's attention through a sensual means.

Pastoring a rapidly growing church which had just purchased land and finishing architectural plans for a beautiful new sanctuary and educational complex to house the multiple programs of community outreach provided by his church, Pastor John was discovered to have fallen to sexual sin. I can't help but wonder what John was thinking as he sat in my waiting room, awaiting his appointment with me. As their pastor, he had referred many of his congregation to me for counseling; now, he was sitting in the same place he had sent others that they might get the needed help to resolve the problems that had encumbered their lives. Finally, it was his turn; I greeted him with a hearty handshake and generically asked him how he was doing. He responded as most new patients do with the meaningless words, "Oh, I'm doing okay under the circumstances that I find myself." Attempting to rescue him from my waiting room to avoid contact with anyone else from our community who might recognize him and begin wondering why he was seeing a Psychologist, I quickly invited him to my office. My compassion for a new patient who has made his or her way to seek treatment is usually easy, but in this case it was most difficult. I was so disappointed that someone whom I had deeply respected and felt had been a co-worker in God's Kingdom had fallen to a level beyond my wildest imagination. To break the discomfort we both felt at that moment, I offered John coffee. Although having had coffee or lunch with him several times before and remembering that he really enjoyed a good cup of coffee, he politely refused, and explained that he had begun experiencing stomach pain and his physician had asked him to decrease caffeine intake.

When we were finally seated comfortably in my office and the door was closed to the outside world, I asked John to join me in an opening prayer as I asked God to take control of the process that would need to happen if John were to reach the goal of complete healing. Following the prayer, I asked John to share with me his version of what had happened in his life and Christian walk that had caused him to compromise what he knew was not pleasing to the God who had called him to the ministry. John began with the recent events on how he had been discovered—not atypical of one telling his or her story to a therapist for the first time. Perhaps it's easier to talk about the recent events rather than look at the root causes or the beginning stages of compromise which led to sin. John reported that his church board had recently approved upgrading the computer systems utilized by the church which would accommodate the projected growth with the new building and expansion of programs. As a part of this upgrade, they felt his computer should also be replaced with a newer model and expanded memory for additional programs he might need in the future. John shared that as the new computer was being installed with current data transferring to the new unit, the computer technician who had been a newcomer to the church, stopped suddenly as he discovered several files and "cookies" from pornographic sites.

John paused in his story as he tried to reposition himself in his chair and reduce the obvious embarrassment that had become apparent in his body language. With some gentle prodding and encouragement from me, he then continued his story; " ... it started one day when I was on the internet searching for some information about a possible vacation for my wife and I ... advertisements started coming up on my screen as I was waiting for the information I was researching ... I began wondering what would happen if I simply clicked on one of these sites ... I rationalized that I was certainly strong enough to get out of that site quickly and that probably nothing else would happen ... Satan reminded me that I was a pastor and convinced me into thinking I was certainly above sin ... I didn't really feel that I would be vulnerable, after all I was ordained and had been a pastor for a number of years ... I began reasoning that it might perhaps make my ministry to men in our church more effective if I knew more about this temptation that so many struggle with ... "

John explained that although he had only spent a few minutes that day and did get out of the web site he had visited, the images that he viewed on the screen seemed to burn their impression in his mind; he shared that he couldn't seem to focus on anything very long without remembering the images he had seen. Although praying for God's forgiveness and feeling reconciled with God, John explained that he remained troubled by the images he continued to see in his mind. He explained, "I desperately prayed that God would take such images from my memory and give me the peace I previously enjoyed in my thought life, but it seemed as if God would not answer my prayer." John continued to explain that several times a day, out of what seemed to be nowhere, an image would re-appear in his mind and cause a complete disruption in his thought process, distracting his attention from the task he was attempting to complete. He explained that he now realized the error of this rationale, but that in desperation he felt that if he re-visited the site maybe then his curiosity would be satisfied and he could put this temptation behind him.

At one of his weaker moments when he knew no one would be at the church to interrupt him, he explained that he re-visited the web site to only fall further into the temptation of viewing the material designed to provoke sexual urges and further exploration of the available material and images. Suddenly, on his screen popped up an e-mail from someone who called herself "Sexy Suzi", inviting him to chat with her. John shared that although in his heart and mind, he knew this would be wrong and that he shouldn't indulge in such an invitation, he yielded to the drive to satisfy his curiosity and plunged even deeper into this sin. Now in addition to viewing the various images on his screen, he began "chatting" with various people on the chat lines, rationalizing that he wasn't doing anything wrong— merely talking to people. John shared that Satan prompted him to see this as a potential form of witnessing to people—perhaps they could call it "Evangelizing Through Chat Rooms." John explained that this further exploration did not satisfy his curiosity or urges, but in fact only strengthened the temptation of which he was finding less strength to avoid. He explained that this process had its own momentum; after the second or third time of hitting those sites on the computer it became much easier. John explained that Satan even helped him come to some rather irrational conclusions that he would be researching this whole area of sexual sin in order that he might better preach against it. John commented, "I was such a fool ... to think that I allowed Satan to not only tempt me in this manner, but then to join him in believing his lies and accept them as rationale ... I can't believe myself ... it was just as if I had lost my rational mind—my thinking was completely irrational!"

The whole process for John from the first encounter with the pornographic website until he was discovered was less than a year—much shorter than most. Perhaps he was less sophisticated than others in covering his tracks, but as I explained to John on that first day of his appointment, his being discovered was probably the greatest blessing that could ever happen as it forced him to face the truth and this very devastating and destructive pattern in his life could be interrupted. Since he was discovered earlier than some, he would have a better chance of saving his marriage and family, hopefully find forgiveness for himself, and be capable of restoration by his denomination which had asked for the voluntary surrender of his ordination credentials. I tried to share with him that his discovery should be viewed as a blessing from God rather than a curse; although he had lost his pastorate, his reputation had been severely damaged, and he might be forced to change careers without the possibility to fulfill the call God had given him to the ministry a number of years before, his soul and ultimate goal of making heaven his eternal home was far more important than these things.

Although still struggling with embarrassment, anger at himself for having fallen to the sin he preached against, and somewhat devastated by the generalized anxiety he felt about the future, he reluctantly agreed to attempt to consider his discovery as being a good thing that had happened. Now the pattern that he couldn't break himself was broken from outside intervention; he vented somewhat over how he felt church leaders could have handled it more graciously with him, but then commented that he understood they were just doing their job and that his anger should really be directed at himself. He expressed much fear over the future of his marriage as he realized that his sin had the potential to wreck his marriage and alter the "All American Family" lifestyle that they had come to enjoy.

What happened in John's situation that allowed him to yield to the temptations that all men will undoubtedly experience sometime in their lifecycle? Is there a predictable cycle that can be identified? Are there some safeguards that can help men or women avoid weakening to such a powerful temptation that is based on the God given sexual drive that was given to man as a blessing? What is the treatment for such problems and once corrected, is it really resolved or is there a risk of it re-occurring? These are all questions John had as we began the treatment process that would help him recover and reach resolution of this problem that had become a very destructive part of his life.

John's treatment began by sharing his story with me; the secrets that he had kept from any one, including his own wife were now being purged by sharing them with a confidante that could help him objectively address the issues that lead him astray. I then asked John if he honestly desired healing from this problem or if he were only participating in therapy under the requirement of his denominational leaders in hopes that he would regain his ordination credentials. This question startled him as he appeared somewhat defensive in his posture—almost angry that I would be so bold to even ask such a question. Observing his reaction, I tried to reassure him by explaining that many patients come to treatment because they wish to have their pain or discomfort decreased. Such patients are really more interested in a "quick fix" so they can feel better. They invest enough to ease the symptoms, but not enough to address the root problem. I further explained such a desire for complete healing as a pre-requisite; God would only heal him if he was genuinely committed just as the paralyzed man in John 5:6 was asked by Jesus, "Do you want to get well?" Complete healing would result only if he was willing to surrender everything to God. John relaxed his posture and affirmed that he desired complete healing more than anything else and that his commitment to his own healing was genuine, no matter what happened to his career or family.

Like so many individuals that come to treatment, John was initially overwhelmed and quite desperate; he knew that the discovery of his sin could alter the entire course of his life and position as an ordained minister. He was anxious to get the problem resolved; he desired to feel better and eliminate the painful emotions of depression, anxiety, and fear that had become characteristic of his daily routine. This was why the critical question of "Do you really want help with this problem?" on that first day of treatment was so important. His investment in conquering this problem, combined with a complete surrender to God's intervention in his life was ultimately the most important step in the entire process of healing. Although responding to this question correctly in that first session, as a psychologist treating this condition, I knew that his answer would be validated or invalidated in the forthcoming sessions as he began to respond to the various steps in the process.

As we closed the initial session, I told John that now that he was clearly committed to complete healing and had accomplished this step as a pre-requisite, we would begin by defining the problem which could lead to a much deeper understanding of the issue, the contributing factors, and subsequent ramifications associated with it. His assignment from that first session was to research the concept of sexual addiction and come up with a relevant definition that we could then discuss in his next session. John agreed to complete this by the next session and anxiously requested how soon we could meet again—a further positive sign of his commitment to address the problem comprehensively and expediently.

John was a few minutes early for his next appointment; it didn't seem to matter to him that others in the waiting room might recognize him as a minister in the community. He used the few minutes while he waited to review his notes from the research he had done that week which lead to his definition of sexual addiction. John was prepared for his session and it appeared that he had completed the assignment thoroughly. He began by sharing a standard definition that Webster's Dictionary provided, " ... a dependence on or commitment to a habit, practice, or habit-forming substance to an extent that its cessation causes trauma." (11) John quickly shared that he hadn't found such a formal definition to be that practical so he started searching the scriptures and his theological resources to create a more relevant definition. From his research of the literature written on this issue, he reported that experts in the field compare it to other addictions such as alcohol or drug dependency where the person has a pathological relationship with a mood-altering chemical. Sex addiction is generally thought to be a person's pathological relationship with mood-altering experiences. For the alcoholic or drug abuser, the chemical becomes central to his life and more important than family, friends, or work. The sexual addict parallels these other addictions as his or her mood altering experiences take on more importance than family, friends, work, and even moral integrity.

After looking at the topic biblically, John shared that he had come to the conclusion that sexual addiction could be concisely defined as the same as original sin since it is the condition of original sin. Using himself as an example, John said he had drifted into becoming "double-minded;" he further explained that he had started trying to satisfy his own sexual urges rather than following God's plan for appropriately satisfying this need. John shared, "I tried to control that which I couldn't control!" John referenced Romans 7:15, 19 in explaining the process by which he was drawn deeper and deeper into the addictive web, "I do not understand what I do ... for what I want to do I do not do, but what I hate I do ... for what I do is not the good I want to do; no, the evil I do not want to do—this I keep on doing ... but it is sin living in me ... ." John had concluded that all sexual addicts were double minded; while perhaps wanting to do better, they hold onto or are trapped by sin.

Looking for my approval, which must have been obvious to John from my positive affirmation of his hard work, he said, "but that's not all that I learned in my assignment ... do we have time for me to share four additional things I've learned about sexual addiction?" I agreed with excitement, reminding him that this was his session and he could share whatever he desired to share with me. John continued by saying, "my reading on this subject has helped me come to four additional conclusions ... (1) as an addict, I have to accept the powerlessness that I have in conquering this problem—I have to rely upon God for helping me correct it, I simply can't do it myself ... I am helpless; (2) all addictions have a progression and get worse, my tolerance to fight off the addictive nature of this behavior weakened each time I participated in it; (3) there is a chemical-biological nature to addictions as the chemical-hormonal process changes in my body, thus making it like what some authors have called a 'powerful high' and it becomes difficult to resist returning to that emotional state; and finally the obvious that I have preached about for years, (4) there are so many negative consequences for it is in fact sin ... I have lost my position as pastor, my self-respect and confidence severely damaged ... I could lose my family and marriage, etc. etc ... ."

In future sessions, John began to examine his family of origin to search for issues that may have contributed in some way to his weakness and ultimate failure to sin. Like many who fall to this sin, John could have easily accepted the notion that his upbringing was in a dysfunctional family and because of this, he weakened and fell to temptation. But John was not looking for the easy way out, when he committed to treatment of this problem in that first session, he became determined to accept responsibility for his own behavior, choices, and now working through the ramifications of those poor decisions. He refused to allow blame to fall on anyone but himself—a very good prognostic sign. Despite my encouragement to examine his family dynamics that may have neglected to teach him about needed boundaries against temptation, he stated, "I have to take responsibility for my choices ... no one is powerful enough to cause me to do anything ... no one caused me to make the decisions I did!"

Unlike many addicts who come from homes where there is a question about unconditional love of the child, John came from a loving Christian home. There was no question in John's mind about his parent's love and support for him; they had encouraged him to fulfill the call to ministry he felt while in late high school, worked hard to financially support his college education at their church's bible college, and proudly attended many of the services where he was given opportunity to preach while in training. He shared that he had no question about his father's faithfulness to his mother; there wasn't any access to pornography in his home while growing up as his parents did not have a computer in his home, nor did they subscribe to any supplemental cable television networks. John shared that he realized from his studies in the area of sexual addictions that many addicts drift into pornography as a means of satisfying unmet nurturance needs from childhood. He further shared that he realized that fantasy often starts out innocently for such individuals and that's why chatting to an unknown person in a chat room becomes so enjoyable as it meets some of these needs.

While sharing that he had read how 81% of sexual addicts were abused as children, a large percentage were abused physically, that almost all are abused emotionally, and that many feel emotionally abandoned by their parents, John adamantly refused to accept any of these reasons for his failure. John concluded that his drifting into fantasy and eventually making decision to engage in this unthinkable behavior was not the result of anything other than his belief that he was invulnerable. He would often comment, "it was my unrealistic notion that I was above the addictive nature of pornography that caused me to slip … Satan validated this lie for me, but I'm not even going to blame Satan for my decision—I must assume responsibility for my choices … I needed to resist Satan rather than allow him to validate my false beliefs that I was strong enough to resist this powerful addictive process … at the time, I allowed my reasoning to become illogical because it eased my conscience and helped me ignore the faithful prodding of the Holy Spirit."

In one session, John shared that in his studies that previous week he had read that the usual process for sexual addition usually involves two steps: (1) thinking or fantasizing thoughts, which lead to (2) acting out the fantasies. John expressed that he now could fully understand why he had been challenged in that first session to see his discovery as a blessing rather than a curse for his discovery quite likely prevented the very likely next step of acting out his fantasies. He realized that had he progressed further, his wife would not have been willing to even consider reconciling their marriage and that his loss would have been much greater. John went on to share that he could now see how people get so hooked on internet chat rooms, "I just clicked on that e-mail message from "Sexy Suzie" and knew I would not converse with her … but I have to admit, it became easier and easier and I started sharing things with her and others that I talked to that I didn't share with my wife … I could be someone other than who I really am while I was in one of those chat rooms … it was much less threatening than sharing with someone face to face … I have to admit that I came to enjoy it and looked forward to opportunities I would have to chat to someone … " John shared that he learned from Suzie or some other person he chatted to regularly that if you wanted to have a private conversation with that person without the risk of others listening in from their computer screen, you could indicate you wanted to "whisper" something to them. By clicking on a specific button, others would then be blocked and the chatting between these two could be given complete privacy. He admitted that as his involvement on the internet grew, his time committed to personal devotions and prayer decreased. Although not openly lying to his wife about the increased time in his office, John confessed that he allowed her to believe it involved work on the building and expansion program for the church. John shared that as he compromised the routine he had once established for his personal devotional time, it became easier and easier for him to engage in his internet activities; as the process continued, he became less troubled about his involvement. John said, "This process where the conscience weakens and stops working to convict you of wrong is what the old timers in my parent's generation use to refer to as "searing the conscience."

One of the many tasks requested of John during his treatment involved having him read and review the theological perspective for the book of Nehemiah since some Christian based recovery programs in sexual addiction utilize this story as a basis for the steps needed in recovery. John came to understand that just like Nehemiah concluded about the walls around the city of Jerusalem had been neglected and had resulted in ruins, the boundaries that once protected him from the temptation and sin of pornography were likewise in ruins. His choices to compromise, which led to addiction, had subsequently caused his life to become ruins! In rebuilding his life, just like Nehemiah rebuilding the walls around Jerusalem, John began to rebuild the appropriate boundaries that had once protected him from the things he had fallen to. Nehemiah had workers begin building the wall in front of their own homes; John began rebuilding with his wife and family—this was far more important than his desire to return to his ministry. John invited his wife to join him in therapy sessions for he desired to reconcile his marriage; in addition to gaining her forgiveness which she had already offered, he desired to begin the slow process of regaining her trust. He seemed to understand this would take considerable time and effort on his part; he pledged his willingness to do anything that she felt would help him accomplish this goal. He committed to never keep any secrets from her. As he shared with her the painful secrets he had kept from her, it was obvious that he was genuine and her feminine intuitive sense seemed to validate the sincerity of his heart.

One of the first tasks assigned them as a couple was what I refer to as a "purging session;" they were asked to set aside a day and get away from home, telephones, cell phones, pagers, and any other means of communication from the outside world. The goal of a purging session is where the "offender" confesses everything to the "offended" and the "offended" can ask any and every question he or she needs to ask to totally understand the offense that was committed. This is a critical step in the healing process and begins the initial steps of rebuilding trust. Although usually quite painful for both parties, it serves to begin the foundation for complete honesty in the relationship; all secrets between them are absolutely purged through this process! As explained to John, without this step in the healing process, his wife would probably continue to have doubt about his total honesty with her; Satan could utilize the missing pieces of information in his confession to stimulate her imagination as she then might imagine things that were probably much worse than what had occurred in reality. John questioned this suggestion and rationalized, "I have hurt her so deeply already, knowing the details would only serve to hurt her more ... !" As further explained to John, Satan could and most likely would use these secrets to continue tempting him. By purging the secrets—every detail of every secret—the private pact with Satan is broken; Satan's influence over John is considerably weakened as he gains strength in overcoming and resisting temptation.

Although the reluctance to take this step was shared by both John and his wife who had initially shared she didn't think she wanted to know any of the details, they both agreed that if this step was required and would help to lead to the healing they both desired for their marriage, they were willing to do it no matter how painful it might be. Although generally after the completion of a purging session, the information discussed at that time can be considered "purged" and doesn't need to be discussed further, John was encouraged to recognize that his wife might at times have some relapses and need reassured that he had told her everything. When questioned by her in the future, he was instructed to see these as "opportunities" to reassure his wife and not become threatened that she didn't believe him when he had painfully told her the details at the purging session. Over the course of time, the doubts eventually subside and such times become fewer and fewer until eventually they disappear.

Just as Nehemiah placed importance on re-building the wall that led to the dung area and so emphasized that this area should be behind a gate and wall, John approached his healing by not only accepting responsibility for allowing the "dung" to become a part of his life, he was determined to remove it and re-build the protective forces that would enable victory over it in the future. He desired that his wife be his primary accountability person and pledged to her that he would never allow a secret to exist between them again. He pledged his faithfulness to her in both his thought life and behavior; he assured her that he had contracted with an internet server that filtered all web sites and even e-mails at the server site and prevented such trash from even entering his screen. He also committed to her that he would share with her any occurrence out of the ordinary that could be interpreted as a temptation for him; he started informing her of every detail of his schedule and when alterations occurred, he would phone her and let her know of the change in plans.

Guiding his progression through therapy, I cautioned John that as he gained momentum in this healing process he could expect an increased level of spiritual warfare—just like when the wall around Jerusalem was half-way built, Nehemiah wisely instructed the workers to work with one hand on the wall construction and the other hand on their weapon to defend against the attacks from the enemy. Beginning each day with personal devotional time, John began re-establishing some protective fences in his own life. He honestly admitted that despite being a pastor and encouraging others about personal devotional time with God, he had allowed his to be neglected—he had allowed this wall to begin crumbling. While their schedules did not allow for devotions together on a daily basis, John and his wife established some special times when just the two of them could pray together; they shared later that these times of sharing together as a couple had taken on new meaning and became a powerful force in the healing of their marriage.

As their sessions progressed, John's wife would at times have relapses and become somewhat depressed as she would think about how the dreams that she had once had for their marriage seemed tarnished by her husband's fall to temptation. She feared what effect it would have on his future ministry and how they would be viewed by others in their denomination, their friends, and, of course, the extended family. Worse than all of these worries, she feared what damage he had done to their children, in their relationship with him as their father. At times, individual sessions were scheduled with her to address her feelings of loneliness, isolation, inadequacy—all very typical reactions experienced by the offended spouse. As she came to realize that her husband's failure was not caused by any inadequacy of her, but a result of his own decision making and allowing sin to become a part of his life, she could re-focus on the tasks of re-building their marriage. Like most men who have fallen to pornography or other forms of sexual immorality, John frequently shared that his wife was a better woman than any of the images he had seen on the computer screen and certainly a better person than anyone he had "chatted with" in a chat room.

After several weeks of therapy and study in between therapy sessions, John shared that he had discovered that most writers in the field of sexual addictions talk about four stages in addiction: (1) Preoccupation—completely engrossed with thoughts of sex which lead the addict on an obsessive search for sexual stimulation; (2) Ritualization—unique special routines that lead up to the sexual behavior which serves to intensify any preoccupation, and adds arousal and excitement; (3) Compulsive sexual behavior—the actual sexual act which is the end goal of the preoccupation and ritualization, and finally, (4) Despair—a feeling of utter hopelessness and powerlessness to change the behavior. John shared that while some men might not fall as quickly as he had done, for him the preoccupation stage occurred rapidly. "Once I clicked on a pornographic site a few times, it was all I could think about ... I couldn't get the images out of my mind, no matter how hard I would try ... I would begin planning for the next opportunity to contemplate this temptation." He shared that his ritualization stage rapidly followed the first stage; he remembered how he would think of reasons to return to his office at the church to pick up materials he had purposefully left or check on agenda for a meeting, or some other excuse he could dream up to rationalize his need to return to his office after hours. John shared that as soon as he got into his car and started toward the church, his excitement would begin mounting and he could feel his heart beat increasing and arousal resulting as he wondered who would be in the chat room that night. Tearfully, John expressed how thankful he was that his compulsive behavior never reached the level of some, where he would have agreed to meet this other person and engage in physical intimacy. He then shared with much remorse, "I guess whether it was physical or emotional—it doesn't matter to God, I committed adultery ... such a fool I was to put my whole life, family, ministry, my personal integrity on the line for a few brief moments of pleasure!" But worse than even the nervous energy surrounding the sexual behavior and ensuring the rational excuses necessary to remain safe from discovery, John said the ultimate despair that resulted after committing the act was at times unbearable. John shared that although knowing this was wrong and feeling unbearable guilt and pain afterward, the process continued due to the sense of powerlessness one has in this cycle. "You see," John added, "I was trying to break the cycle on my own ... I thought I could conquer it ... I didn't think I could ask God to help me get out of something I got myself into ... I was so ashamed that I didn't feel worthy of God's help—but ultimately I would never break out of this pattern without surrendering it to God and realizing my powerlessness!"

In conjunction with all the other parts of his therapy, John had committed to study further the pitfalls of the internet and increase his knowledge about safeguards—both for his own safety and hopefully that he might someday be able to share with others through his ministry. Unfortunately, many Christians and even members of the clergy are very naïve about the inner workings of this industry. John spoke with several internet server companies and read several materials on how this technology works. He shared how outraged he had become when discovering that web sites utilize what is called a "cookie" or special browser file stored on the computer system that enables them to recognize who you are and when you visit. Microsoft's Internet Explorer 5 will save any site's cookie file on your computer and automatically send that same file back to the site whenever it is hit again. This cookie file stores such personal information as your name, billing information for a site you buy products from, and similar data. By default, Microsoft's Netscape Navigator, which is the software utilized on most computer systems for accessing the Internet, accepts all cookies without issuing a warning that it is doing so. While becoming extremely angry by what John described as an invasion of his privacy, he shared that now he understood how once he had clicked on that first website, the cookie that was established then provided that website and others necessary data to solicit him further as they saw his interest in their website.

One of the many goals for John's psychotherapy sessions involved an expansion of his knowledge concerning this whole area of sexual addiction and why many are so vulnerable to this form of media. Our discussions on this topic helped him see how the pornographic images were perhaps more of a threat to males than to females as men tend to be more visually stimulated; and, therefore sexually provocative visual materials tend to feed the sexual urges God created in mankind. On the other hand, women tend to be more tempted to engage in "chat rooms" since their acting out is more emotional or relational in nature. Admitting that he had assumed that this problem was predominately one for males, John shared that he was surprised to learn about the rapidly increasing numbers of females who had become involved in internet chat rooms. Starting as innocently chatting with someone on the internet, the process can rapidly progress toward what some writers are calling "cyber sex" and then agreeing to meet in person. While cyber sex is defined as "using computerized text, images, or sound files for sexual stimulation," an "internet affair" utilizes interactive computer chat to create exchanges for the purpose of sexually arousing oneself and others with such activity often culminating in mutual masturbation. (12) These so called, internet affairs involve emotional sharing with others and romantic involvement which should be reserved for their spouses. The sharing rapidly progresses from innocent sharing of interests to more personal and private things. Some who study this problem suggest that "anonymity on the Internet leads to emotional and sexual engagements beyond what people do in face-to-face encounters—even with their spouses." (13) John seemed surprised to hear that studies are now showing that women are as likely to engage in cyber-affairs as men; and, that many of these individuals have never experienced either an emotional or sexual affair outside their marriage. Perhaps these internet affairs are facilitated by ease of convenience, getting needed "validation" from others, the false notion that just talking to someone else isn't adultery, and as some have rationalized "an opportunity to be someone you don't feel you are in reality."

As you might suspect by this time in John's story, he and his wife did finally reach the goal of healing largely due to their hard work together, John's willingness to accept full responsibility for his sin and express total remorse for his wrong, and finally their openness to allowing God to provide the healing they both desperately needed. John had taken a non-ministerial position at a local firm where he worked for a couple of years as they completed treatment; they found a local church where they attended faithfully and participated in many of the ministries provided by the church. As they continued to progress through treatment, it was becoming obvious to me that God had brought complete healing to John, his wife, and his family. He was enjoying his layman's role in the church and the secular position which gave him more time with his family and friends; however, lest he become too comfortable in these roles, I asked him one day at the conclusion of his session to begin praying about God's timing of re-entering the ministry. His stunned look at me clearly suggested he was extremely apprehensive about the process involved with regaining ordination from his denomination. Breaking the silence between us, I expressed my validation of him by saying, "John, you are called into the ministry ... you made a mistake common to mankind ... you expressed complete remorse, you were forgiven by God, your wife, your family, and others concerned ... after God forgave you, He justified you; you have completed treatment and in my professional judgment, you have resolved the issues concerned ... you are ready to complete the calling that God placed on your life."

John agreed to discuss this matter with his wife and that the two of them would begin praying for God's direction for this decision. Several days later, I met with John and his wife; they expressed with excitement but with much apprehension their decision to apply for re-ordination. I validated their decision as I handed them a report that I had already prepared for his denominational leadership verifying he had completed treatment and that I was recommending re-ordination. Within weeks, John was re-ordained by his denomination and the couple received and accepted a call to a church some distance from where they had been living. John had a very successful pastorate at that church and it was followed by two other churches where his ministry has continued to flourish. Occasionally, I hear from them or see them at a conference; they not only report victory—they exemplify the healing that only God can do in such situations. They display a deep happiness, peace, and contentment that have clearly enriched their lives and ministry. Their oldest son is now in college preparing for the ministry; and their daughter, who is completing her junior year in high school, is seriously seeking God's direction in what she has begun to feel might be a call to the mission field. John has been very instrumental in ministering to multitudes of men and women in his congregations about the necessities of firm boundaries on internet services; he also serves as an executive officer on a community action organization to prevent pornographic media from becoming available to the local town where they reside and pastor. May God be exalted for the healing He brought to this precious couple.

Chapter 13

Divorce—Is It Ever Right?

B eth was a 38 year old, married, mother of three children who had contacted my office for an appointment after talking with several of her friends and on one occasion her pastor. The reason for her appointment was to discuss the frustration with her marriage and consideration of a divorce from her husband. Beth was a Christian and attended one of the local churches not far from my office. Several of her friends as well as her pastor had given her my name; to accommodate them, she had agreed to see me in marital counseling prior to making any final decision about the future of her marriage. Beth came alone for the first appointment but figured that I would ask her to invite her husband for the next one.

Having handled an emergency just minutes prior to Beth's scheduled time, I apologized to her for the brief wait she had in the waiting room as I introduced myself and invited her to my office. She was cordial and expressed that she understood. Although offered coffee or tea as a means of helping her relax on this first contact with me, Beth refused, saying she had stopped drinking as much caffeine since it had begun to bother her stomach. Once seated comfortably in my office and after I had taken a few minutes to review the information she had written on the registration forms describing her presenting problems, I asked, "Beth, can you tell me more about the reasons you requested an appointment today?"

Beth responded slowly with some caution, "Well, I've been married for eighteen years and my husband and I have three children, a son fifteen years old, and two daughters, one seven and the other five. My husband works as an estimator for a large construction firm in town and spends very little time at home with me and the kids ... he works on Sundays and doesn't go to church with us ... I think I have lost my love for him as a husband ... I feel like a single parent with a brother living with us!" Pausing for a moment to assess my reaction to what she was saying, she then continued, "A few months ago, after remaining lonely and frustrated for a number of years now, I decided I couldn't live this way any longer ... I started doing things with other women in the church and tried to establish my own support system. I haven't been unfaithful to him, but we really have no relationship at all ... I feel numb ... I don't think that I love him ... perhaps I never did love him! He seems married to his work; even when he is home in an evening, his version of spending time with the family is to sit in the family room with us while we are watching television and he is working at a card table doing paperwork for his job."

Sensing that Beth was building a case for asking my position on divorce, I asked her, "So what have you been thinking about doing to help solve this problem?"

Beth responded, "Well my pastor told me that I don't have biblical grounds for a divorce ... he agrees that we don't have the kind of marriage God intended for us to have, he said as he interprets scripture, I can't divorce my husband since I don't have biblical grounds."

"What have your friends advised?" I asked.

In response to my question, Beth said, "Some express the same opinion as the pastor, but others share my frustration and say that I deserve better than this ... that God wants me to be happy."

Trying to remain non-judgmental since I knew this lady would not return to my office for a second session if I responded in any manner that could be interpreted negatively by her, I responded, "Let's talk further about the marriage, your husband's lack of understanding of your legitimate needs, perhaps look at the history of your marriage to see if we can find any clues as to what went wrong and if things could be corrected now."

Over the last several years of practice, I have seen many persons—both men and women, who have had initial sessions like Beth's. They are contemplating divorce but recognize they don't clearly have biblical grounds to divorce their spouse. Similar to Beth, they often have gone to their pastor who has not given them permission to divorce; in some cases, the pastor has judged them severely and without even hearing their pain or attempting to encourage they seek counseling, will tell them should they divorce they would be sinning. In rare instances, some pastors have threatened to excommunicate them from the church should they chose to follow through on divorce. Beth's pastor had wisely referred her for counseling to look at the dynamics in her marriage that might be affecting her husband's behavior, her unhappiness in the relationship, and explore any possible resolution to these matters rather than divorce. When failing to obtain her pastor's approval, Beth followed up with some of her close friends to try to build a case or feel validated in her thinking that divorce would be acceptable; they too responded in a manner that didn't clearly support her position and thus caused her to further question her motives. Beth was seeking validation from some legitimate source that would help her justify doing what she knew was probably not God's will for her life.

Like most individuals who are frustrated in their marriage, Beth had accepted the modern day, secular notion that if the marriage isn't working, then you dispense with it and start over. The challenge that was before me as a Psychologist was to demonstrate a compassion for Beth's pain while helping her examine all the issues, ramifications, and explore possible solutions to this problem without appearing judgmental in any way. The minute a patient senses that his or her therapist is judgmental, the rapport and respect they may have for that clinician is diminished if not completely destroyed; further assistance toward reaching a resolution is stifled and quite often the patient drops out of treatment. Based on the information Beth presented in our first meeting, I agreed with her pastor that it appeared she didn't have biblical grounds for divorce; however, I knew that to express that at this juncture would be premature and not sensitive. Rather than express my feeling prematurely, I focused more on the pain that Beth was experiencing and tried to validate that marriage is suppose to be more than what she had experienced. Her children likewise needed a father figure more than her husband had provided them. I validated that both Beth and her children were certainly suffering from what appeared to be a "workaholic" husband and father. I validated Beth for seeking counseling by saying, "Beth, I admire you for seeking counseling ... whatever decision you eventually make regarding this problem, you will feel better if you know you have made every effort possible, including counseling, to save your marriage."

I asked if Beth thought that her husband would come in for either a joint session or an individual one. She affirmed that she thought he would, as he seemed desperate in the last few days after she had told him she was thinking of leaving the marriage. A second appointment was made; he agreed to come to that session with Beth. Beth's husband, Dave, was a nice looking man who had just turned forty a few weeks before. After some initial small talk about turning forty and I was sure a good rapport had been established, I asked, "Dave, what do you feel are some of the problems in your marriage?"

Dave responded, "I know I work too many hours and I'm trying to cut back some; however, I have to bring a lot of work home if I want to keep this job ... I hope it gets better ... but at least I have a secure job when others are losing their jobs." Further discussion with Dave revealed that he was a man who was deeply committed to his family; while he loved both his wife and children, he lacked understanding of how to express it to them. He worked hard to provide them with all the "extras" to which they had grown accustomed; he literally expressed his love for them by providing for them materially. He had been reared in a home without much emotion demonstrated and seemed deficient in his understanding of his wife and children's emotional needs.

As is typical in marital cases like Dave and Beth, I asked them to complete an assignment for their next session. I explained that they were quite aware of problems in the marriage and it was because of these things, they started thinking about the need for counseling.

As an assignment, I asked them to individually make a list of the minimal things that would need to change in the marriage for them to be happy; additionally, I requested they make a second list of strengths or positive things in their marriage or with their spouse. The two lists were to contain the same number of items so that each weakness or problem area would also be linked with a strength or positive. This approach is often used to force a couple to think about the positive things along with the negative and serves to approach things in a more balanced manner rather than just focusing on all the negatives. Couples in a stressful marriage often have forgotten the strengths or the positives they have together, as they are so focused on the problems; it's also the strengths that can often be used to help resolve or alter the problem areas.

The next session took place a few days later; both Dave and Beth came with their assignment completed. The two lists were combined and one list of problem areas was formulated with the idea that these would become our treatment goals. As predicted, looking at the strengths became a bit more challenging for both. Beth and Dave had not focused much on the positives in the recent days of their marriage. Subsequent sessions were scheduled and some progress was made on the list of goals we had established. Throughout the course of therapy, which involved several weeks, I gently tried to incorporate what I believed the Bible says about divorce and marriage. We talked about the verses of scripture found in Ephesians 5 that provide a guide for God's plan of marriage. We also discussed I Peter 3 that talks about God's plan for the husband and the wife, and the different needs expressed by men and women as a result of gender differences. Despite rather healthy discussions in our sessions and commitments from Dave to spend more time with his wife and kids, there was not much change in marital dynamics. Beth continued to spend time with her female friends from church as she felt she needed their fellowship and Dave continued working many hours beyond his scheduled time. Unfortunately, she was becoming more comfortable with the less time spent at home; she had also consulted some of her non-Christian friends for their advice. From her comments in the sessions, it appeared she was gaining momentum for validating her decision to divorce her husband. When Beth started talking in session about possible divorce and asking for clarification of things they should be saying to the children to help prepare them for the ultimate breakup of the family, I asked Beth if she felt she had biblical grounds for divorce and if she could legitimately say she had prayed earnestly for God's direction on this decision. Although claiming she had done this, I rather doubted that God would give her permission to divorce her husband without clear biblical grounds.

At this time in their therapy, Beth announced that she had planned a brief vacation for her and the kids; they were going to spend a week at her parent's farm in another state. While she and the kids were on this vacation, Dave felt compelled to stay home and catch up on paperwork and quarterly reports, which were overdue. In an individual session with Beth prior to their departure, she shared that she had pretty much come to the decision for divorce and that if things didn't miraculously change; she would be filing for divorce upon her return from vacation. She had planned to use this time to share her decision with her parents and give some thinking to how she would present it to the kids after returning home. My heart sank as only a therapist can experience when a patient is deciding on something you know in your heart is not appropriate.

Let's digress from Beth and Dave's story for a time to discuss the whole concept of divorce and if it is ever permissible. Some would take a very legalistic view concerning divorce and from this would very narrowly define sexual adultery to be the only legitimate condition under which God would permit divorce. As a psychologist, I have had numerous cases over the years of clinical practice that involved women who felt trapped in abusive marriages where their husbands were physically abusing them and their children, but felt they could not divorce since he had not committed sexual adultery. These women had often been misadvised and misdirected by well meaning persons and pastors who were taking a legalistic view on divorce. Many were advised to stay in dangerous home situations where their husbands regularly placed their lives in danger under the influence of drugs and alcohol. Despite my encouragement and counsel, they chose to stay in such situations for fear that to leave or divorce would be sin and unpleasing to God.

Others would take such a liberal view that they define anything as adultery and therefore justify divorce much like the secular world does. In these cases, I have often become frustrated by a lack of willingness on the patient's part to look objectively at defining adultery. It would appear that they are using the right terminology to justify their decision; however, just because one chooses to define a situation or refer to it in a certain manner doesn't justify the decision. One can choose to believe a lie or false doctrine in an effort to gain support for their decision, but God judges the heart and can clearly detect the motive of such a person. As a psychologist, I have heard a multitude of liberal interpretations of adultery; some are actually quite humorous (i.e. "I feel that God brought this woman into my life to fulfill my sexual needs ... God wants me as His child to be happy!"). While they may feel justified and even supported by peers since they have chosen to articulate the situation by using the right words, they will still stand before a holy God some day and give an account of their choices. Unfortunately, God will define as sin many of the excuses used to rationalize their inappropriate decisions.

Both extremes are wrong; somewhere in the middle of these two positions, there is a more balanced view and it most likely has the component that our Savior Jesus Christ modeled so well in his ministry on earth—grace. While many churches were content to keep quiet about the matter of divorce for a number of years since there were few if any divorced persons within the congregation, this is no longer possible as the trends have changed drastically. Experts studying divorce trends among groups of people are finding that Christians now divorce at about the same rate as non-Christians. One study (1) conducted by a Christian Psychologist by the name of Tom Whitenen, revealed that while incompatibility was the predominant reason given by non-Christians for divorce, adultery and abuse were the predominant reasons given by the Christian group of divorced persons. Dr. Whitenen's research further concludes that Christians tend to take marriage more seriously and are more apt to delay the decision for divorce; however, ultimately those who end up divorcing do so after tolerating more pain from spousal abuse, abandonment, and/or adultery.

In a sermon series (2) on divorce at Crossroads Church in Circleville, Ohio in June of 2003, Senior Pastor Lonnie Potts addresses the issue of divorce comprehensively. Pastor Potts explains that there are only four voices in all of scripture that addresses the issue of divorce—Jesus Christ, Moses, Paul, and of course the group who always had something to say about such matters, the Pharisees. In introducing this subject and the position he feels should be taken by the Church concerning it, Pastor Potts clearly states that God's perfect will for everyone is a lifelong, monogamous, heterosexual marriage relationship. Man was created for companionship and with needs that can be fulfilled through marriage. Jesus was always pro-marriage and anti-divorce; however, while divorce is not God's perfect will for mankind, there are some occasions where He permits divorce. In answering the Pharisees trick question to Jesus in Matthew 19:4 (" ... is it lawful for a man to divorce his wife for any and every reason?"), Jesus references Moses by responding, " ... what God has joined together, let man not separate" (Matthew 19:6). God's will for any marriage is that it be a lifelong commitment and certainly all measures to correct problems that could lead to divorce must be taken.

Scripturally, it would appear that divorce would be permitted legitimately in only three conditions: sexual adultery or immorality, abuse, and abandonment. Moses speaks to the issue of <u>abuse</u> as referenced in Matt 19:8, Jesus speaks to the issue of <u>adultery</u> in Matthew 19:9, and finally Paul speaks to the issue of <u>abandonment</u> in I Corinthians 7. As a psychologist, these three causal factors would be seen as clinically sound reasons that a patient should seriously consider divorce as an option if there are no signs of remorse or a repentant heart on the part of a spouse committing these acts of unfaithfulness. Of course, this does not mean that one should immediately or impulsively choose divorce as an option when a spouse has made a mistake or fallen to temptation if there is genuine remorse and a commitment to resolve or correct those conditions that may have contributed toward such behaviors. Since

God's perfect will would be to bring healing to the broken relationship and He does to multitudes of couples experiencing this trauma, efforts at attempting reconciliation must be made in most situations! However, if the offending partner attempts to rationalize, justify, or blame others for the inappropriate decision making, or otherwise refuses to take responsibility for his or her behavior, these would be good clinical signs of insufficient remorse or guilt. In such cases, the lack of remorse or accepting responsibility is a precursor for repeating the same pattern of behavior. Despite promises to change and somewhat insincere attempts at apologizing, the pattern will likely repeat itself and further hurt and pain results to the victim spouse.

The first voice speaking on divorce was Moses who is referenced in Matthew 19:8, "Moses, permitted you to divorce your wives because your hearts were hard." Moses legitimized divorce on the grounds of abuse. (3) In that day, Jewish law and practices permitted husbands to divorce their wives for anything the husband disliked and even very slight pretenses. With this cultural practice, men had become abusive to their wives and frequently mistreated them. In an effort to prevent men from abusing or putting their wives out inappropriately, Moses took the stand that divorce could only be legitimized if there was abuse and then only with an official process. This was Moses' attempt to protect the wives from abuse at the hand of their husbands. Mosaic law required that the man establish grounds or reason for divorcing his wife rather than enacting this on the basis of any whim. After the woman was set free with a writing of divorcement, the man could not bring her back into his home to continue abusing her. These precepts, given to Moses by God, were intended to regulate the law of divorce in the Christian Church. It is never God's will that someone stay in a truly abusive relationship; however, many well meaning Christians have advised women to stay with their abusive husbands in hope that he would find Christ. God does not expect us to risk our lives or the lives of our children by staying in such relationships. Once again, we must understand an accurate definition of abuse rather than call minor disagreements or normal arguments abusive. While verbally attacking each other in a marriage is certainly harmful to that relationship and should be discouraged as an unhealthy means of communication, this is not considered the abuse that Moses referred to when he legitimized divorce on the grounds of abuse.

Abuse appears in the literature to have three forms: physical, sexual, and emotional or mental. Physical abuse is perhaps the easiest of the three to distinguish as there are usually externally observed signs of physical injury such as bruises, blackened eyes, burns, lacerations or abrasions, missing or loosened teeth, skeletal injures, head injuries, and even internal injures at times. Sexual abuse is usually more secretive and not easily observed by the outsider to the couple's relationship. It quite often involves demanding one's sexual partner to participate in sexual activities that are uncomfortable or demeaning in nature. The source or cause for sexual abuse often appears to be the result of one's exposure to pornographic media. After reading written materials, watching videos, viewing images on the Internet, or having some other exposure to pornographic stimuli, the man or woman introduces such ideas and fantasy to the marital bed. Rather than the marital union being the blessing that God created it to be within marriage, it becomes defiled. Hebrews 13:4 warns against this defilement, "Marriage should be honored by all, and the marriage bed kept pure, for God will judge the adulterer and all the sexually immoral." Sexual abuse is relatively difficult to detect outside the clinical setting since the physical trauma is not exposed and the victim is reluctant or even fearful to reveal the abuse to anyone, even close friends or family. Emotional abuse, like sexual abuse, is more difficult to observe. It is usually related to a multitude of negative interactions, both verbal and non-verbal, that accumulate over time. It may involve harsh words, adverse criticism or condemnation, degrading comments about a person or their attributes, or simply emotionally withdrawing from one's spouse. Emotional abuse can leave the victim with a sense of rejection and lowered self-esteem as a result of the accumulation and cycle of continual degrading comments.

The second voice speaking on divorce was Jesus Christ who in Matthew 19:8 said, " ... If anyone who divorces his wife, except for marital unfaithfulness, and marries another woman commits adultery..." Adultery was regarded as a great social wrong as well as a great sin in Biblical times. The adulterer was a man who had illicit intercourse with a married or engaged woman and such a woman was considered an adulteress. Intercourse between unmarried persons was considered fornication and thus sinful. Here we see that Jesus accepted divorce only on the basis of sexual immorality. According to Pastor Potts, sexual immorality comes from the Greek word "pornea" which means pornography (4). If one acts out sexually with someone other than their spouse, develops rather destructive habits of sexual aberration or other sexually perverse activities, then that person would be considered to be living a sexually immoral life which Jesus would consider adultery and thus acceptable grounds for divorce. Such a person has broken the marriage covenant; and thus, frees his spouse for divorce and re-marriage.

The third voice heard on the subject of divorce is Paul who permitted divorce on the basis of abandonment in I Corinthians 7:15, "... if the unbeliever leaves, let him do so ... a believing man or woman is not bound in such circumstances ... God has called us to live in peace." This provision is only given after commanding the husband or wife who is a believer to remain with his or her unbelieving spouse if that spouse has not abandoned the marriage covenant. In such cases, the believer positively influences the unbelieving spouse and the children from that union. While every effort must be made to reconcile differences and remain married, if the unbelieving partner has chosen to abandon his or her spouse and lacks remorse or a willingness to change such behavior, then, according to Paul, divorce is permitted due to abandonment.

While many might quickly indicate their spouse has abandoned them and thus justify their intention or desire to divorce their spouse, perhaps further study of abandonment is necessary. Abandonment is defined as "... to forsake utterly; desert; to give up on; discontinue; withdraw from; a complete surrender to natural impulses without restraint or moderation; to leave completely and finally; freedom from constraint." (5). Abandonment is not and cannot become the justification for divorce when a wife says her husband doesn't seem to understand her emotional needs and as a result causes frustration for her in the marriage. Newlyweds are often quite inexperienced and lack maturity; the initial years of marriage will have many challenges as the two people merge different backgrounds and experiences into one. Disagreements and misunderstandings are normal and do not represent abandonment— even if the spouse withdraws emotionally for a time to think about the conflict or ways to resolve their differences. It is also quite commonplace to see husbands or wives want to continue their involvement with peers after marrying and perhaps initially spend too much time with those activities at the expense of spending time with each other. For example, the husband who wishes to continue spending excessive amounts of time with his college buddies in sports activities or the wife who wishes to continue her involvement with college roommates in shopping trips or attending concerts. These activities or even spending some time with peers is not wrong; however, if these things take precedence over the time spent with each other in the marriage, the balance is missing and after some time, the spouse begins feeling neglected. It would only become abandonment when these kinds of activities became excessive and a repetitive pattern of disregard for changing the behavior despite pleas from the spouse who feels neglected. In such cases, obviously the couple should seek professional help through marital counseling to reconcile such differences.

According to Genesis 2:18-24, marriage was instituted in Paradise prior to the fall; this would be considered the original charter of marriage and the basis on which all regulations regarding marriage should be framed. God corrected many false notions that existed on the subject of marriage in Matthew 22:23-30, and placed it as a divine institution which is ordained by God. Marriage was described as "honorable" in Hebrews 13:4 and the prohibition of it is noted as one of the signs of degenerate times in I Timothy 4:3. The duties of a husband and wife are clarified in Ephesians 5:22-33, Colossians 3:18-19, and I Peter 3:1-7. The marriage relationship is used to represent the union between God and his people in Isaiah 54:5; in Ephesians 5:25-27 marriage is used to illustrate the love of Christ for his saints.

Consistent with Pastor Pott's interpretation of the scriptures concerning biblical grounds for divorce, we recognize adultery, abuse, and abandonment as clinically sound or legitimate reasons to consider divorce. This position would be considered a balance between a legalistic perspective and the other extreme of liberalism. While divorce should never be the first line of attack, there are certain conditions where divorce appears to be the right choice. To avoid being misled or misdirected by others concerning the decision for divorce, patients are encouraged to "test the spirits" as we are told to do in I John 4:1, "...do not believe every spirit, but test the spirits to see whether they are from God, because many false prophets have gone out into the world." Ultimately, no one, neither pastor nor clinician, can be the perfect adviser or have all the answers in such matters as complicated as a decision for divorce. While Godly counsel and a comprehensive review of scriptural grounds is helpful, the patient should only come to the final decision after prayerfully considering all of the relevant issues and ramifications to their decision.

Now let's return to my patients—Beth and Dave—and get "the rest of the story." You will remember that Beth had decided to take a vacation with the kids to visit her parents in another state while Dave stayed home to catch up on the workload in the construction company where he worked. Beth planned on telling her parents of her decision to divorce Dave and use the time to plan how she would share this news with their children. In that last session prior to her departure, I asked her if she would be willing to do one thing for me while on vacation. She agreed, as she wanted to have my support for the decision she would make. Taking a real risk as I had no clinical rationale for saying what I was about to say, but discerned that it was the right thing to say, I asked, "Beth, would you promise me that you will get alone with God for fifteen or twenty minutes each day of your vacation and have prayer— perhaps as a part of your individual devotional time?"

Puzzled somewhat, she said, "Sure, I can do that ... but is there a particular reason you are asking me to do this?"

"Yes, there is a very important reason, Beth." I replied. Giving further explanation, I added, "I really feel you still have some questions about whether divorce is the right choice for you and

Dave. I sense that you may be acting out of frustration, years of loneliness, and unhappiness. You have lost hope of ever experiencing a happy marriage and you don't see your husband changing the way you would like to see him change."

"Well, you are probably right … but don't try to talk me out of my decision; I have thought a long time and I'm rapidly coming to a conclusion … I'm just exhausted and want to get on with my life!" she replied.

To this comment I responded, "Beth, I realize you have not impulsively made this choice, but I know you will not want to have any regrets about the decision in a few years—like many of my patients who have divorced. I just think you should give a few more days of concentrated prayer that God will either heal your marriage and give you hope that you will regain happiness or give you clear assurance that you have biblical grounds for divorce and therefore free you from the marriage."

"Are you questioning whether I have biblical grounds for divorce, Dr. Miller?" asked Beth.

After a pause to allow Beth to wonder what I was thinking, I cautiously responded, "I really can't be the judge of that, Beth. I think that only God can confirm that your husband has committed adultery, abused you in some manner, or abandoned you … and even then, unless he doesn't demonstrate remorse or isn't willing to change, could you really justify divorce on biblical grounds … but you will have to seek God's confirmation on these things. I do really feel that God wants you to be happy as his child, and that he will either heal your marriage if you both desire that healing or give you validation that you can divorce your husband."

Beth quickly responded, "But Dr. Miller, I don't feel any love for him any longer … I feel numb … I don't hate him and I wouldn't want anything bad to happen to him, but I just don't feel any affection for him … he feels more like a brother to me than a husband."

Again after some hesitation and thought to model for Beth the seriousness of my response, I reiterated, "This is why I would like for you to get alone for a few minutes each day … you could go to the barn, back yard, or some other place away from the others so you can be alone with God. During this prayer time, ask God to either heal your marriage or give you permission to divorce your husband. I believe that God could heal your marriage and if He does, He will restore a love for your husband that you may have never experienced before. If God chooses not to heal your marriage, then I believe He will give you a definite confirmation that divorce is acceptable and we can then begin helping you and your family through that process."

This is not a risk I take often with patients for fear that they will hear what they wish to hear and think it is from God, therefore returning to the next session indicating that God has given them permission to do what they had already planned to do. But I felt led to say these things to Beth. She agreed to follow my request and committed to have a time of prayer each morning prior to the day's activities beginning.

While she was gone, I had a couple of sessions with Dave. I worked hard at helping him understand how Beth really needed his affirmation, was missing his romance, and if he didn't shape up soon, he was probably going to lose her even though he was a loyal husband. He responded by sending her roses to the farm one day, called her and the kids a couple of times and wrote a couple of notes to insert with cards as well. Although planning a welcome home party with some of her friends at church, as Satan would have it, her return flight was delayed so his plans for the party were in vain as the flight arrived too late and her friends had gone home. But as I told him, his motive was right and demonstrated a significant change in his priorities; Beth would not be able to ignore these efforts. It was my hope and prayer that God would use these things to soften Beth's heart to His voice and sincerely seek God's will rather than respond to notions expressed by secular friends.

A few days after her return home, both Dave and Beth were scheduled for a joint session. Although having not planned a family session, they brought their two daughters with them for the session. My heart sank when I saw the two daughters with them in the waiting room; I assumed their presence indicated that Beth had made her decision for divorce and she would be telling them in today's session that the family unit as they knew it would be changing.

Those are always very stressful sessions to watch children react to such news; they usually respond with a multitude of emotions as their parents tell them that they have decided to divorce. I am deeply saddened to watch children attempt to process such news; their home, which they thought would always offer them security and safety throughout their life is changing before their very eyes. The worst part of this process is to sense the hopelessness and helplessness the children feel in this situation. As a therapist, you want to make it better for them but realize you are as helpless as the children in altering the decision.

I asked Beth and Dave if they would like to see me initially prior to inviting their daughters to join us in the session. Beth responded, "Oh, I don't think that will be necessary; they can join us now if it is okay." I agreed but still felt somewhat confused by her response; she had always before been concerned about how to share the divorce with her daughters and wanted assurance that we would do it in a manner that would minimize their hurt and pain. I wondered if Beth had just come to that point of decision-making and was aggressively forging ahead as I often see happen in such situations.

I was relieved somewhat when I saw the expression on both Dave and Beth's face; it was different than I had seen in a number of sessions before this one. They appeared less depressed and perhaps somewhat relieved—possibly even happy. Anticipating the confusion that my nonverbal behavior was conveying, Beth announced, "Dr. Miller, several things have happened in the last few days; and we have made several changes in our home. Dave has talked with his boss about needing to work fewer hours and they decided to hire an assistant for him so he can be home with me and the girls more. The girls and I really missed him on our last vacation, and we want to plan another trip soon for all of us ... Dave hasn't had a vacation in the last three years and his boss wants him to take some time off as soon as he gets his assistant up and running."

By this time, I had concluded that Beth had decided to reconcile the marriage. With much relief, I asked the two girls, "Girls, is there something different about mommy and daddy or your home?" Beth and Dave appeared somewhat nervous as we all waited for their response.

With a big smile on her face, the younger of the two who was completely uninhibited, which really made her parents concerned about what she might report, piped up and said, "Yep!"

Thinking that she might talk about Daddy and Mommy "kissing" or "hugging" more, I asked, "What's different?"

She responded, "My daddy is going to go to church with me from now on ... he doesn't have to work on Sundays anymore!" I complimented Dave for this commitment and told the girls that I was sure they would be mighty proud to have their whole family attend church together. I then excused the girls for a few minutes so I could discuss some "adult" things with their parents. After the girls had left the therapy room, I asked Beth to describe what had happened to change things so drastically in their marriage.

As she took Dave's hand, she responded to my question tearfully by saying, "You remember when you asked me to have fifteen minutes of prayer time each day ... you know to get alone with God and ask Him to either heal my marriage or give me a definite answer that would allow me to divorce?"

I responded, "Yes ... I remember. Did you do that?"

Beth said, "I really didn't think that anything would help, but I wanted to keep my promise to you and felt that I owed it to you as you had tried to help us through this ordeal and we would need your help with the girls if we did divorce. So, I reluctantly complied at first. I got up before the others and went out to the barn—where I use to play growing up on that farm. It was so peaceful there during the early hours. I did just what you asked me to do—I prayed that God would either heal my marriage or give me permission to divorce my husband. I poured my heart out to God, sharing my desperation due to the loneliness and unhappiness I experienced. Well, the real change in my position came when God seemed to ask me to begin loving my husband as He loved him ... and, Dr. Miller, I don't think that I have ever loved Dave in that manner! As I began to look at the positives in our marriage and the many attributes that Dave has, I began experiencing a much deeper love for him. I see things entirely different now ... I'm falling back into love with my husband!"

God did heal Dave and Beth's marriage; and, fifteen years later, they are still together today. Their children are all grown and on their own; teenage years with their oldest daughter was quite trying and challenging, but their marriage was solid and they operated as a team, supporting each other through those challenging years with her. As "empty nesters" now, they have a good marriage and frequently spend time with their children and grandchildren; they are also actively involved in their local church. Although Beth almost fell into the trap of deciding on a divorce and trying to justify it, she knew in her heart that she did not have biblical grounds for divorce and that she would not be in the perfect will of God by divorcing her husband. Because she was open to God's voice and willing to change her thinking, God miraculously healed her marriage.

Endnotes

Chapter 1 What Are The Critical Spiritual Issues of Today?

Chapter 2 Important Boundaries For a Life of Holiness

1. Keith Drury, "The Anatomy of Adultery," *Money, Sex, & Spiritual Power,* Indianapolis: Wesley Press, 1992, 45.

Chapter 3 Anger—Is it Wrong?

1. Elizabeth A. Lemerise & Kenneth A. Dodge, "The Development of Anger and Hostile Interactions," Chapter 37 in *Handbook of Emotions.* ed. Michael Lewis & Jeannette M. Haviland (New York: The Guilford Press, 1993, 317).
2. Random House Webster's College Dictionary, New York: Random House, Inc., 1995.
3. Ibid., 1995.
4. Ibid., 1995.
5. Ibid., 1995.
6. Marlin Hotle, "Forgiveness," Circleville: *Mount of Praise Camp Meeting Sermon.* August, 1998.
7. Thomas Hermiz, "Get Rid of All Bitterness" Circleville: *Mount of Praise Camp Meeting Sermon.* August 1997.
8. Julie, "Excerpt From Personal Diary of Julie" Columbus: 1987.

Chapter 4 Anxiety—Is it Sin?

1. J. Mark Shadoan & Lynnette L. Shadoan, "Treatment Planner," American Association of Christian Counselors. Forest: AACC, 1999.
2. Frank Minirth & Paul Meier, *Happiness Is A Choice*. Grand Rapids: Baker Book House, 1991.

Chapter 5 Proper Self Esteen vs. Selfish Pride

1. Random House Webster's College Dictionary. New York: Random House, Inc., 1995.
2. Ibid., 1995.
3. Ibid., 1995.
4. Ibid., 1995.
5. Thomas Hermiz, "Self Love," Circleville: *Mount of Praise Camp Meeting Sermon*. August, 1997.

Chapter 6 Solutions For Dealing With Guilt

1. Frank Minirth & Paul Meier, *Happiness Is A Choice*. Grand Rapids, Baker Book House, 1991.
2. Random House Webster's College Dictionary. New York: Random House, Inc., 1995.
3. Ibid., 1995.

Chapter 7 The Importance of Balance and Proper Priorities

1. Jeanne Anselmo, RN, "Stress Management & Biofeedback" *Healthy Life Guide*, (Pamphlet developed as a promotional for the office of Family & Psychological Services, Columbus: 1998).
2. Positive Promotions, (Pamphlet developed as promotional for stress management practice), The Positive Line # 79930, Flushing: Positive Promotions., 2000.

Chapter 8 Good Decision Making

Chapter 9 The Importance of Learning How to Forgive

1. Random House Webster's College Dictionary, New York: Random House, Inc., 1995.
2. Marlin Hotle, "Forgiveness," Circleville: *Mount of Praise Camp Meeting Sermon*, August 1998.

Chapter 10 Perfectionism—Is it an Emotional Problem or a Sign of Holiness?

Chapter 11 Sexual Identity Problems—Is There a Cause? What's the Cure?

Chapter 12 Internet Pornography—Newest Threat to the Church & Family

1. Eric Tiansay, "Porn Pastors," *New Man*. Psalm Coast: Strang Communications, September/October, 2992, 23.
2. Ibid., 23.
3. Mark Laaser, "A Husband's sexual sins," *Shine Magazine*. Weatherford: Shine Media, March/April, 2992, 75.
4. Stephen Arterburn, "Protecting Your Child From Pornography," *Christian Counseling Today*. 11, 1, 2003, 32.
5. see http://covenanteyes.com/addictionsigns.php
6. Ibid.
7. Ibid.
8. Stephen Arterburn, 33.
9. Ibid., 33.
10. Mark Laser, 75.
11. Random House Webster's College Dictionary, New York: Random House, Inc., 1995.
12. David Schnarch & Ruth Morehouse, "Relationships in Cyberspace," *Family Therapy Magazine,* September/October, 1, 5, 2002, 15.
13. Ibid., 16.

Chapter 13 Divorce—Is it Ever Appropriate?

1. John Huffman, Jr. ed., *The Family You Want.* Christian Focus Publication, 2001, 134.
2. Lonnie Potts, "What Does God's Word Say About Divorce?" Circleville: Crossroads Church Sermon Series, June, 2003.
3. Ibid., 2003.
4. Ibid., 2003.
5. Random House Webster's College Dictionary, New York: Random House, Inc., 1995.

Printed in the United States
44618LVS00003B/7